Ulysses S. Grant

⤙✦ *An Album* ✦⤚

Other Books by William S. McFeely

Yankee Stepfather:
General O. O. Howard and the Freedmen

Grant: A Biography

Frederick Douglass

Sapelo's People:
A Long Walk into Freedom

Proximity to Death

Ulysses S. Grant

◂◂ *An Album* ▸▸

WARRIOR, HUSBAND, TRAVELER, "EMANCIPATOR," WRITER

William S. McFeely

Photographic Research by
Neil Giordano

W. W. NORTON & COMPANY
NEW YORK ✷ LONDON

Book design by Lovedog Studio
Production manager: Andrew Marasia

Library of Congress Cataloging-in-Publication Data

McFeely, William S.
Ulysses S. Grant : an album / William S. McFeely ; photographic
research by Neil Giordano.—1st ed.
p. cm.
ISBN 0-393-02032-0 (hardcover)
1. Grant, Ulysses S. (Ulysses Simpson), 1822–1885. 2. Grant, Ulysses S. (Ulysses Simpson),
1822–1885—Pictorial works. 3. Presidents—United States—Biography. 4. Presidents—
United States—Pictorial works. I. Giordano, Neil. II. Title.
E672.M155 2003
973.8'2'092—dc21

2003003681

W. W. Norton & Company, Inc., 500 Fifth Avenue, New York, N.Y. 10110
www.wwnorton.com

W. W. Norton & Company Ltd., Castle House, 75/76 Wells Street, London W1T 3QT

1 2 3 4 5 6 7 8 9 0

To my students and the tabletops on which we crawled across Civil War battlefields

Contents

Introduction

Cadet Ulysses S. Grant's favorite course at West Point was drawing. His work was well done, and his excellent visual sense stood him in good stead during the Civil War. I have always thought that if cancer hadn't killed him at sixty-three, he might have found respite from the frustrations of peacetime life as an amateur artist. There were professional artists who went to work on the battlefields of the Civil War; the drawings of Alfred Waud and Winslow Homer are excellent, as is the work of some of the soldiers, whose sketchbooks are still turning up.

There were practitioners of another artistic genre, photography, hard at work during the war and indeed throughout Grant's whole lifetime. With the plethora of technology available to us today that has made photographing the world remarkably sophisticated, there is a tendency to see nineteenth-century photography as primitive. It was, after all, born only short decades before pioneers of outdoor photography gave us the remarkable images of the Crimean War and then our Civil War. But these were accomplished with a large-view camera, mounted on an oaken tripod with brass fittings and requiring large glass-plate negatives. The photographer needed a pack mule to carry this heavy equipment to the battlefield. Action was displayed only by accident, as while generals sat still for the necessary long exposure, supply wagons rolled past them in a blur.

There was nothing primitive about what could be accomplished when the subject did sit still, often with a hidden post behind to steady the head and body and, perhaps, a pocket to hide hands hard to keep from moving. In fact, Timothy O'Sullivan, Alexander Gardner, and Matthew Brady (who also put together a remarkably talented team) produced images of great artistic distinction. The portrait of Grant, on the dust jacket and repeated in this book, and that of Julia Fish, also included, are of the highest caliber of portrait photography.

Few of the pictures in this book are of that quality, and many are steel engravings of photographs (there was not yet a method for printing photographs in newspapers), but they encompass the whole of Ulysses Grant's life. This book has the rather grand subtitle *An Album*, but in many ways a synonym, "scrapbook," might have done as well for the Grants. There are images here of just the kind that someone in the Grant family might have pasted into a memory book.

I have had a good time letting my own memory work again on Grant. When I finished my *Grant: A Biography* I put him and his war aside. When a book is complete, I feel the need to move on, often to a very different subject. But enough time has elapsed now that it has been fun to think about him again. There have been other biographies of Grant by writers with different views of the man, but when there was a recent reprinting of my book, I was happy to let it stand as is. Ulysses Grant is a fascinating man, as were his times, and I have enjoyed thinking of them both in light of where we stand today.

Ulysses S. Grant

An Album

⟶ 1 ⟶

"Attributed to Slavery"

Grant and the Meaning of the Civil War

Ulysses S. Grant opens the final chapter of his *Personal Memoirs*, his masterful account of the Civil War written at the very end of his life, with this assessment: "The cause of the great War of the Rebellion against the United States will have to be attributed to slavery."[1] If there is a bit of begrudging in the "have to be," Grant is unequivocal in naming the single cause. It was slavery, the way of life of most black Americans before the war. With the end of Grant's war they were free. Twelve years later, in 1877, on his trip around the world, thousands of parading workmen in the industrial north of England had saluted him as "the Great Emancipator," as the general who had liberated millions of America's workers. As president of the United States, he had proved the only president for nearly a century to confront directly the question of what that freedom should mean.

---

1. Ulysses S. Grant, *Personal Memoirs of U. S. Grant*, 2 vols. (New York: Charles L. Webster, 1885), 2:542.

And yet, in the final two sentences of the chapter closing his *Memoirs*, he left a different legacy. Generously referring to the outpouring of sympathy as he was known to be dying, Grant unwittingly suggests how the concern for black Americans came to be swept under the nation's rug for seven long decades ahead. He writes: "It is a significant and gratifying fact that Confederates should have joined heartily in this spontaneous move. I hope the good feeling inaugurated may continue to the end."[2]

Grant was referring both to a widespread general sentiment, North and South, and specifically to the Confederate generals who joined

Union generals in making the trip to Mt. McGregor, outside Saratoga Springs, New York, to pay their respects to the dying warrior. One who came was Simon Bolivar Buckner (*left*), Grant's close friend in his early army days and the wartime foe who had received Grant's demand for unconditional surrender after his Confederate force was defeated at Fort Donelson. Now, leaving Grant's deathbed, Buckner, no longer regarding his old friend's wartime severity as unchivalrous, told reporters that the moment of their parting was too sacred for him to describe. The Southerner's emotion was entirely genuine, as was that of others. Indeed, it could be said more broadly that among the nation's gentlemen, the rancor of the war was behind them. Reconciliation was possible now that the two regions of the country no longer divided over slavery, over race. White gentlemen were as one again.

It is Ulysses S. Grant's ironic fate that his life illustrates both sides of the great divide that has prevailed in American history over what the Civil War meant. His sentences, not far apart in his memoir, speak precisely to the point historian David Blight in *Race and Reunion* has so brilliantly made.

2. Ibid., 554.

HARPER'S WEEKLY.

A

JOURNAL OF CIVILIZATION.

VOL. VI.—No. 270.]   NEW YORK, SATURDAY, MARCH 1, 1862.   [SINGLE COPIES SIX CENTS.
[$2.50 PER YEAR IN ADVANCE.

Entered according to Act of Congress, in the Year 1862, by Harper & Brothers, in the Clerk's Office of the District Court for the Southern District of New York.

THE SURRENDER OF FORT DONELSON, FEBRUARY 16, 1862.—[SEE NEXT PAGE.]

Fort Donelson, where Grant required "unconditional surrender" by his friend Simon Bolivar Buckner, C.S.A.

There have been those who remembered as Grant did that it was slavery that caused the war. Abraham Lincoln had defined the war when at Gettysburg to honor the dead, he reasserted the Declaration of Independence's most telling line, "all men are created equal." With these words, Lincoln ennobled the Emancipation Proclamation that he had signed earlier in 1863, ending slavery wherever the war took his armies. Once the war was over, the question the nation faced was, what will be the place in society of the former slaves? There were those who took Lincoln's words to mean what they said. And there were those whose emphatic goal was seeing to it that those words would not mean what they said. The resumption of white supremacy, no longer achieved through enslavement, was what they sought. This purpose was cloaked in the more admirable aim of reuniting the nation.

It is often suggested that the nation was so engrossed in other interests, such as making money, that it forgot about the freed people. It would be more accurate to reverse the matter and say that once the slavery question had been decided, the country could busy itself with other pursuits.

African Americans were boldly active in achieving their liberation and rejoiced in their emancipation. They were plainly in sight in the war's immediate aftermath, when the attention was no longer on their slavery but on them—and their struggle for a safe, successful place in the society. This struggle was the challenge that Grant would face as president. Before he reached the White House in 1869, much had been begun. The Freedmen's Bureau gave immediate welfare aid, oversaw the redistribution of lands that Congress enacted, and aided the opening of schools.

Faced with the violence of those who would frustrate these advances, Congress, over President Andrew Johnson's veto, established five military districts in the former Confederacy to protect the freed people. Black men served in all levels of civil government. The Fourteenth Amendment seemed to guarantee the freed people's citizenship; the Fifteenth the freed men's vote. What had not been taken into account was the strength that white supremacists would muster to frustrate these gains. By the 1870s, they had returned to the legislatures that they had previously boycotted, and with terrorist tactics, used on an ad hoc local basis or organized by the Ku Klux Klan, and politically adroit maneuvering that was sustained by the nation's Supreme Court, the white supremacists rendered both the Fourteenth and Fifteenth Amendments useless to the very people they were designed to aid. The military presence in the South ended and with it all attempts of federal enforcement of the rights of African Americans.

The poverty of the defeated South contributed mightily to the plight of the freed people, as the majority of former slaves had nowhere to turn economically other than to the virtual peonage of sharecropping and the lien system that kept them perpetually in debt. Reconstruction failed.

But this is to get ahead of our story. When Grant was elected president in 1868, failure was not assured. A war hero of immense popularity who was grudgingly admired even by those he had defeated, Grant headed the Republican Party, the architect of whatever federal gains the freed people had made. The party was in a majority in both houses of Congress, while the Supreme Court was composed of a majority of justices appointed by President Lincoln. The opportunity for action on behalf of the freed people existed.

Grant espoused the Fifteenth Amendment, ratified during his first term, which explicitly stated that race could be no barrier to voting (for which he was rewarded with African American votes for reelection in 1872). Grant also authorized an assault on the Ku Klux Klan. And yet, when he left office in 1877, the freed people were less secure than when he had entered it, and he knew it. The compromise that allowed for the choice of his successor, Rutherford B. Hayes, was achieved when Northern Republicans abdicated their concern for tormented black citizens in exchange for the White House. For decades, historians told their students a distorted story of Reconstruction, one that totally obscured black achievement. In this version of the postwar nation, the white South, ignobly treated by the victorious North, had suffered under the oppressive rule of Northerner exploiters and incompetent blacks.

Reconciliation became the laudable aim. The nation's social revolution was replaced with the task of reunion. Binding the wounds of war was to be the theme of our history until black Americans led a second try at reconstructing the country seven decades later. Until then, black Americans were invisible.

Had they always been invisible for Grant? He had worked side by side with slaves on the house they built and in the fields of his Missouri farm in the 1850s, and so, certainly he knew these black men. Whether

Hardscrabble.

that experience translated into a concern for the millions of other people who were slaves is not clear in his prewar letters. Did he see the millions of enslaved laborers in his own slave-state world as clearly as he saw other suppressed people he encountered? He was remarkably clear sighted as he reported home on the plight of Mexican peasants caught between two armies during the Mexican War. Similarly, after the war, when stationed in the Far West, he appreciated, as many of his fellow peacetime soldiers did not, the plight of Native Americans. They came down the valley of the Columbia River, refugees driven from their lands to the east by emigrating white settlers. They were destitute and bewildered, and Grant, who himself was deeply troubled, noticed.

It was as war refugees that black Americans came vividly into focus for him. Caught between two marauding armies, people clung to the

FORT VANCOUVER, W. T.

outside of trains taking the retreating Union army back to Memphis. Those who weren't pushed off the trains, or who had walked or had come in wagons, lived in destitution on the freezing streets of Memphis in January 1863. Grant ordered John Eaton, a humane and sensible chaplain, to look after their welfare. He proved a social worker, rather than a warden.

Grant welcomed the recruiting of African Americans into the service following the Emancipation Proclamation of 1863. He regarded them as well motivated to fight in a war that would end their and their people's slavery. The photographs beginning on page 10 illustrate not only the remarkable progress that the freed people achieved, but also the problem of subsistence that they faced. In the first picture, taken near the end of the war a black Union soldier stands next to the ruined

A Union soldier at Richmond slave pens.

A confident Union soldier.

slave pens in Richmond. The contrasting images of the Union soldier in his nation's uniform and those pens could not be more striking. The next evocative photograph (*left*) from the Chicago Historical Society's collection suggests how effective the nation's racial blinders would become. I am not sure that we have in subsequent American art another image of an African American young man of such innocent confidence. Winslow Homer's black subjects are certainly powerfully rendered, but they are somehow uneasy in their grace. In contrast, the men John Singer Sargent portrayed are often undoubtedly handsome, but rendered more as objects of sexual desire than as portraits of independent men.

There are many illustrations of black regiments, particularly of the Massachusetts Fifty-fourth of Fort Wagner fame, but also, for example, of the First Carolina Volunteers, composed of former slaves. These were made

The United States Navy. Note the black faces.

up of black enlisted men and noncommissioned officers; the officers were white. But note the scene of the deck of a Union ship in 1864 (*above*). The sailor so clearly in view in the center foreground is not the only African American on board. Look closely at the men farther to the rear. They are not the servants ready to serve meals to white men that we might see in pictures taken aboard ship during most of the following century of our fiercely segregated United States Navy.

More typical is the picture of black men—and a woman—doing manual labor to support the war effort (page 12). Posed as it is, the picture is difficult to interpret, but there is a tend-to-the-job attitude, rather than a servile appearance, to these workers. Interesting in contrast is an illustration from *Harper's Illustrated Weekly* showing black laborers in the huge, immensely taxing—and ultimately futile—task of digging a canal that General Grant hoped would redirect the unruly Mississippi River (page 13). Note that the foreman directing, indeed enforcing, the task also appears to be a black man. That river has always

A party of workmen.

had a mind of its own. When the canal scheme failed, Union gunboats successfully ran the gauntlet of Vicksburg's guns. That spectacular maneuver is recorded in a famous Currier and Ives print; the canal diggers' picture went the way of old newspapers.

If the war allowed more than two hundred thousand African American soldiers to take a great step toward freedom, back home the immense task was simply subsisting, as the picture on page 14 of a woman standing on bleak land next to a bleak cabin so clearly illustrates. She, at least, may have been holding on to what had long been, for better or worse, home. An overwhelming number of freed people hoped for land of their own, often the land they had worked as slaves. On page 15 (*top*) is a group of people ready to start their lives as free Americans.

Other freed people, uprooted by the devastation the war caused in their part of the nation, were, at the war's end, living in what look desperately like the displaced persons' camps of the twentieth and twenty-

A useless canal dug by hand.

GRANT AND THE
MEANING OF THE
CIVIL WAR

· · · ·

13

Gaunt, but this woman has a relatively prosperous home.

first centuries' wars (opposite, *bottom*). For many, the restoration of a family torn apart by sale was an immediate goal. Often these attempts, documented by poignant advertisements for lost kin in black newspapers, were fruitless, but the result of searches near to home were more successful. There are countless pictures of groupings of families, frequently extended families made up of members taken in after a forced separation from their own blood kin (page 16).

Help for them was promised by the Freedmen's Bureau, created at the end of the war and charged by Congress with distributing to the freedmen lands abandoned by their rebel owners. When white former landowners protested to a sympathetic President Andrew Johnson, state governments in the South, sanctioned by Johnson, passed Black Codes restricting their African American citizens. Private citizens, with acts of violence and threats of more, were terrorizing the freed people. Johnson further eroded the former slaves' hold on their independence by restoring lands to the white planters that the freedmen had begun working on their own.

In 1866, Congress took action to protect the freed people who were eager to move ahead with their new status. Schools were in great

A family of free people.

Refugees in a shanty town.

Ready to face the world.

demand. Deprived of education as slaves, they knew the power of the word and were eager to achieve it. Adults as well as children filled new schoolhouses, as seen in the illustration on page 17.

Over the opposition of President Andrew Johnson, Congress, to thwart the resurgent rebels and to protect the freed people who were often in danger of their lives, passed measures requiring new state constitutions that called for Negro enfranchisement. On one remote Georgia island, people who as slaves had been force-marched to the interior to get them out of the way of blockading Union gunboats, found themselves, in 1864, in the path of General William Tecumseh Sherman's vast invading army. Over one hundred of them, war refugees, walked back to the coast and, with the ending of the war, were granted parcels of land on the island that was the only home they had known. In the spring of 1865, independent farmers now—they had not been confronted with losing the land to its former owners—they organized a school, in 1866 a church, and in 1867, the men lined up to register to

"ZION" SCHOOL FOR COLORED CHILDREN, CHARLESTON, SOUTH CAROLINA.—From a Sketch by A. R. Waud.—[See Page 790.]

A South Carolina school.

vote. The illustration on page 18 shows listeners intent on the word of a politician.

Recent historians credit Grant with a better record on racial matters than some of us have observed. Such a reappraisal is based on his winning the Civil War, of course. But he is also given high marks for such personal actions as freeing his sole slave or his presidential achievement of the Fifteenth Amendment or his forceful attack on the Ku Klux Klan, which momentarily curtailed its activities. But, this reappraisal seems more a matter of well-meaning white observers patting Grant on the back. Disappointed black Americans at the time—or now—might see that things had gone from bad to worse in the eight years Grant was in the White House.

In Grant's defense, the hoary plea of inevitability is invoked. Most of the nation, not just the South, was racist. Public opinion was running against black people and their problems. "The times," that other standard villain, were against him. But is it so certain that an

ELECTIONEERING AT THE SOUTH.—Sketched by W. L. Sheppard.—[See Page 467.]

Eager voters.

immensely popular war hero who, after all, had the reputation for getting things done could not have achieved more to secure African Americans than he did? Grant, with his eye always on the object of victory during the war, had no such determination when it came to achieving either dependable security for the freed people or their full civil rights.

Grant did not have the voice of a Lincoln, but his very reticence at the podium was compelling in its own way. If the anachronistic word "charisma" does not apply, this short, stocky, strong-silent-type man was a compelling presence. At the Civil War's end, Grant was the emanci-

A thoughtful, stalwart soldier.

pator to black Americans quite as much as Lincoln. Had Grant carried that flag and championed the freed people at every turn, it would have been more difficult for the racists to pursue their course. What might have happened if he had identified himself more strongly with the Republican parties in the South who sent their candidates, both white and black, to local offices, state legislatures, the judicial bench, and to the national Congress? As he had in the war, he could have had his eye on an eventual goal of security and achievement for the freedmen and pursued it, despite setbacks, all the way to its Appomattox.

Grant's tenacity had won a war; it just might have won the peace. But tenacity was the very problem. In the first place, there is no way to minimize the determination, the tenacity of the advocates of white supremacy. And yet, had Grant applied his own remarkable version of that trait, it might have made a difference. But that tenacity never came into play during his presidency. Instead, it got seriously misplaced by his quixotic, sustained determination to annex Santo Domingo. This pursuit cost him the allegiance of the admittedly trying but powerful Senator Charles Sumner, who was the one true champion of the freed people in the Senate. Grant's secretary of state, Hamilton Fish, noted in his diary an absence of continuity in the president's concern for the freed people. Upset one week by an outrageous and lethal attack on a meeting of black citizens, Grant, by the next cabinet meeting, would seem to have forgotten about the matter—and would have taken no action.

Similarly, Grant surrounded himself in his cabinet with men who had little or no concern for the freed people. One who did, John A. Rawlins (*opposite*), his wartime chief of staff and then secretary of war, died in September 1869, during Grant's first year in office. Even when in Amos Akerman he found the best attorney general for dealing with racial questions that the nation was to have for a century and sustained him in an all-out attack on the Ku Klux Klan, Grant capitulated to pressure. Whether pressured by furious white supremacists or equally frustrated railroad entrepreneurs, whose dubious dealings Akerman was also onto, Grant fired him after a year on the job.

To be sure, white public opinion was turning against the freedmen. Even if Grant had been as steadfast as he had been at war, he would still have been up against formidable obstacles. It would be difficult to overestimate the importance of newspapers and periodicals in this period, and vivid cartoons both shaped and reflected popular attitudes

John A. Rawlins.

(see pages 22–24). These appeared in publications published in New York City. Racism was rampant. Grant had neither the will nor the way to shout it down.

Once out of the White House and, indeed, out of the country on his worldwide trip, he could see his mistakes. In 1878, on shipboard, Grant told a reporter: "Looking back . . . over the whole policy of reconstruction, it seems to me that the wisest thing would have been to have continued for some time the military rule. Sensible Southern men see now that there was no government so frugal, so just, so fair as what they had under our generals. . . . Military rule would have been just to all, to the negro who wanted freedom, the white man who wanted protection, the Northern man who wanted Union." Grant, as many Northerners had

GRANT'S NEW WAR HORSE.

Note the vicious rendering of an animalistic black man and the
scatological pose of the Chinese man.

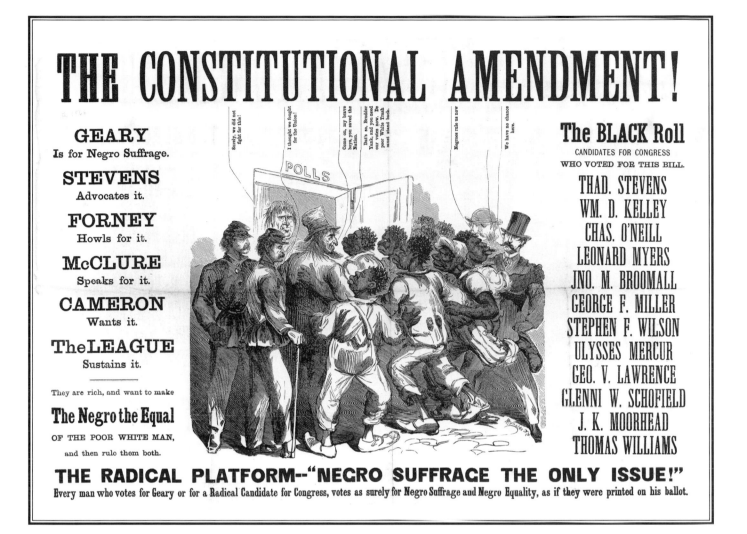

How welcome are the voters from page 18?

One view of Reconstruction politics.

chosen not to do, had become a realist as to the result of the Fifteenth Amendment. It had not done the job it was intended to do. "It was unjust to the negro to throw upon him the responsibilities of citizenship, and expect him to be on even terms with his neighbor."[3] The recently freed people were, in effect, expected to use their even more recently given vote to insure their own safety as well as their civil rights, a task the federal government thereby relinquished. By the end of his presidency, Grant had come to see that this approach had failed. It had taken into account neither the political adroitness of the white supremacists nor their effective use of terrorist tactics.

Grant also spoke of his general disappointment with the way the South had turned out since the war—there had been less emigration from the North of ambitious working-class people and little repudiation of the views of the secessionists by Southern working-class people. The racial climate of the South had not changed. The result of the acceptance by the Southern states of the Fifteenth Amendment "was unjust to the North. In giving the South negro suffrage, we have given the old slave-holders forty votes in the electoral college. They keep these votes, but disfranchise the negroes. That is one of the gravest mistakes in the policy of reconstruction."[4]

Grant, more than he may have realized, was predicting that for decades white supremacy would hold sway in the South, while the North succumbed to the self-induced conscience-soothing amnesia that settled over the white land. Black Americans lost what they had worked so hard to gain. It was upward of a century before another president would recognize and attempt to remedy the injustice.

Seven years later, Grant had a new preoccupation. There are, in my view, few more triumphant personal redemptions in American history than that achieved by Ulysses Grant, out of office and dying. Battered and bruised by the workings of both politics and commerce, Grant, knowing he had a cancer that would kill him, wrote, in ten months, a literary and historical masterpiece, his *Personal Memoirs*.

As I have indicated in my essay in this book, the writing of the *Memoirs* was a great personal accomplishment. The photograph on page 26 of him on the porch, pad and pencil in hand, working on the

3. Quoted in John Russell Young, *Around the World with General Grant*, 2 vols. (New York: American News Co., 1879), 2:362.
4. Quoted in ibid.

Grant at work on his memoirs in the summer in 1885.

Copyrighted July 22 '85

Grant during the week before his death and Harrison Tyrell ready to care for him.

manuscript to within days of his death, attests to his determination. Grant might not have grasped the irony that in another photograph of him reading on the porch (*above*), his black servant, Harrison Tyrell, is almost lost in the dark of the doorway. As with the slaves who worked with him on the house he called Hardscrabble, so Ulysses Grant's private tie with Harrison Tyrell may have been of the finest. But in light of the nation's history, there is a telling symbolism in the black man nearly invisible as the white man is justifiably bright with honor.

2

Love Story

Julia and Ulyss

Julia Grant needs rescuing. She was in many ways a silly woman, more unsure of herself than she would admit. I suspect that she gave her husband some bad advice when he was president. She was the devoted helpmate of her illustrious husband, but not in the obsequious way that the phrase suggests. Julia was more than that; the whole woman was of a very different dimension. We have been looking in the wrong corners to find Julia at her best. She had strengths to match her faults.

When I began work on *Grant: A Biography*, I wanted to make it a study of Julia as well as of Ulysses Grant. I gave up the idea when it was clear that the sources dictated that it would be a lopsided book. With a vast amount of material on the general and president and a paucity of the pieces of paper that would enable me to make a full person of his wife, there was no way to do justice to her. Not even the most personal of documents, their letters to each other, were balanced. Julia kept Ulysses's excellent letters; they give a wonderful look at his character and ideas. He did not keep her letters to him.

The Personal Memoirs of Julia Dent Grant, only published in 1975, three quarters of a century after she wrote them, stands in vivid contrast to her husband's *Personal Memoirs of U. S. Grant*, published in 1885. Reinforcing stereotypes, hers are romantically feminine, his sternly masculine. Compare, for example, his prose to hers: "My family is American, and has been for generations, in all its branches, direct and collateral," are Ulysses's opening words.[1] Julia's read: "My first recollections in life reach back a long way, more than three-score and ten now. We, my gentle mother and my two little brothers, were on the south end of the front piazza at our old home, White Haven. We had just arrived. Dear papa, coming out with seeming great pleasure, caught me up and held me high in the air, telling me to look, the very trees were welcoming me."[2]

Ulysses Grant has laid a cornerstone for his book. He states an ancestry any American of his day could be proud of (and skillfully avoids having to say how that seemingly sturdy family fared through what were, in fact, often declining fortunes over the seven, by my count, generations preceding Ulysses's.) The author has staked a claim for a solid past and, implicitly, invited no doubts as to the firmness of his own fortunes prior to the Civil War.

Julia's book, on the other hand, is filigreed. After quoting the standard cliché for the average life span, which she has exceeded, she gives her narrative the scent of magnolias. There is something just too gentle about that "gentle" mother. Julia has ascribed to her mother, and to herself, a china-doll image of the perfectly domesticated female removed from the responsibilities and ugliness of the masculine world. Her relationship to that mother was more complex than the adjective "gentle" admits. In Julia's description, Ellen Wrenshall Dent is placed with three of her children on the commodious porch of a house grand enough to bear the name White Haven, outside St. Louis. Julia took great pride in her family and their plantation home. Her father, of whom she was greatly fond, greets her by lifting her toward the mur-

1. U. S. Grant, *Personal Memoirs*, 1:17.
2. Julia Dent Grant, *The Personal Memoirs of Julia Dent Grant*, ed. John Y. Simon (New York: G. P. Putnam, 1975), 33.

muring treetops in a wholly idyllic moment. Julia painted the family's country place just outside St. Louis as Edenic, no less so for the garden tended by slaves. In her account, she carefully adds that they were well provided for in the best (if mythic) Southern planter tradition. Her readers would know that having "servants" to care for her confirmed her gentility.

Only rarely and obliquely did she face up to realities that belied her claims to glamour. One of her "colored maids," when dressing her, once said, "Oh, young missus, you are looking mighty pretty, but you never come up to Old Missus in looks."[3] This nice bit of psychological rebellion on the part of the slave must have hit home. Julia was not as good-looking as her mother or her younger sister. She had an incurably stocky figure, was chinless, and had strabismus, a malady that made her right eye move up and down constantly and with uncontrollable regularity. Ulysses saw past the romantic mirage to a woman whose strengths defied gossamer wrappings.

"One of my superstitions had always been when I started to go anywhere, or do anything, not to turn back, or stop until the thing intended was accomplished." Ulysses Grant might have been describing himself during the Civil War, but instead he is recalling, nearly forty years later, in 1885, how as a young second lieutenant at his first posting, Jefferson Barracks, he set

Grant fresh from West Point.

out alone to see his lady. "I did not know the way, depending upon making inquiries on the road, and if I got past the place without knowing it, instead of turning back, I would go until the road was found turning in the right direction, take that, and come in by the other side. So I struck into the stream, and in an instant the horse was swimming and being carried down by the current. I turned the horse's head towards the other bank and soon reached it."[4] Ulysses Grant was firm, the horse swam, and he made his way directly to White Haven, to Julia.

Julia Dent's brother Fred, also stationed at Jefferson Barracks, outside St. Louis, had brought his West Point roommate home to nearby White Haven to meet his family. The Dents' country place was grander than any Grant had known, but he came back not to sit on its veranda, but to see one of Fred Dent's sisters, Julia. She was equally drawn to the shy, slight, pleasant-looking young man. Theirs was not to be an over-the-fan eye-batting flirtation. What they found they had in common was horses. Riding and simply being with the animals had been Grant's passion—"passion" being not too strong a word—since he was a small boy. She, defying the standards of the Southern belle she had been brought up to be, loved the back of a horse too. "After that first visit he became a daily visitor. Such delightful rides we all used to take! The Lieutenant rode a bonny little brown steed with flowing mane and tail. He called him Fashion. My horse was a beauty, a chestnut brown, and as glossy as satin, and such pretty ears and great eyes. She was part Arabian, and I named her Psyche. Such rides! in the early spring, the tender young foliage scarcely throwing a shadow. Well, I cannot tell of those two winged moments. He was always by my side, walking and riding," Julia recorded in the finest and characteristically romantic passage of her *Memoir*.[5]

Theirs was to be a protracted courtship of four years. Ulysses soon was ordered to Louisiana, then to Texas, and finally into war in Mexico. Julia waited until his return, and in 1848 they were married. Except when Ulysses's military duty interfered, the two were together for the whole of their thirty-seven-year marriage. If there is more than a touch of fluff in her prose, it does not disguise the deeply sensuous nature of their courtship.

Julia, despite her romantic claims to fashionable femininity, was a

4. U. S. Grant, *Personal Memoirs*, 1:50.
5. Julia Grant, *Personal Memoirs*, 48.

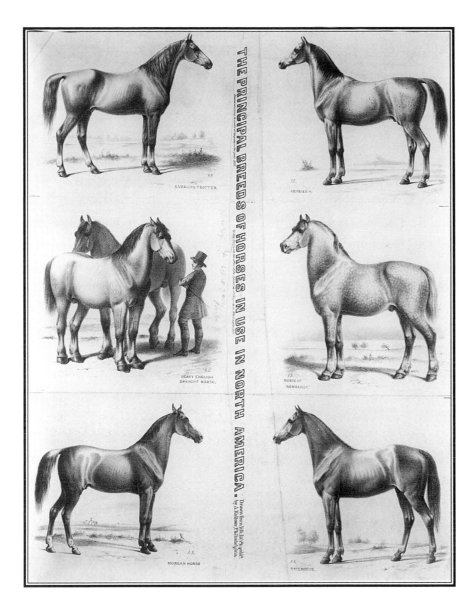

strong, athletic woman. A yarn has come down through the family, and was told to me by her great-granddaughter, about how long after she had given up riding and been encased in first lady satins, she and Ulysses were sitting on the porch of their cottage in Long Branch when one of the boys came out and, scorning the steps, vaulted over the fence to the yard below. Amused, Grant said, "Julia, what would you do if the porch had no steps and the house was on fire?" She said not a word, but got up, grasped the railing with two hands, cleared the fence, and landed down on the grass.

She was strong in other ways. She bore four children, lost none, and, until weight and lack of exercise (of which she was capable) got the better of her lungs, she was virtually without illness for the whole of her seventy-six years. She was strong in her emotional attachment to her husband as well. She went with him as the dutiful army wife when he was given a new post at the Madison Barracks in the far northern reaches of New York State. She badly wanted to accompany him to still another post, this time at Fort Vancouver, in the truly remote Oregon Country. (Grant rightly said no. Julia was pregnant with their second child. Had she gone with her husband, she would have been traveling across the Isthmus of Panama during a yellow fever outbreak on the day the baby was born.)

Ulysses barely endured this, the most disastrous period of his life. He suffered from severe depression, drank, and had to leave the army. His letters to her were heartbreaking. It has never been clear how she fared in this time, but his letters, responding to hers, suggest that she was floundering without him. They recovered. Their third child, a daughter, Nellie, was born exactly nine months after they were reunited.

With her family looking over her shoulder, Julia stood by her husband as his farm on her father's land failed. She arranged a job for him with a cousin of hers, but bill collecting was the last thing he was cut out to do. They shared real poverty; one Christmas he had to pawn his watch to buy her a Christmas present. She moved with him to Galena, Illinois, after he had endured the humiliation of begging his father for a job in the family leather goods store, working for his younger brother. All of this demanded strength and determined loyalty on Julia's part. It was only when he was thirty-nine that the Civil War rescued the Grants from obscurity.

St. Louis, Dec 23rd 1857

I this day consign to J. S. FRELIGH, at my own risk from loss or damage by thieves or fire, to sell on commission, price not limited, 1 Gold Hunting Detached Lever & Gold chain

on which said Freligh has advanced Twenty two Dollars. And I hereby fully authorize and empower said Freligh to sell at public or private sale the above mentioned property to pay said advance—if the same is not paid to said Freligh, or these conditions renewed by paying charges, on or before Jan 23/58

U. S. Grant

Even during the war, Ulysses Grant took sustenance from his immediate family, Julia and their four children: Fred, named after her father and brother; Ulysses, Jr.; Nellie, given her grandmother's and aunt's name, Ellen; and, finally, Jesse, named after his father's father. Below are Jesse and Nellie as children at about the Civil War's end, and on page 36 is Nellie as a young girl. There are attractive stories of Grant getting down on the floor to roughhouse with the boys. At Cold Harbor, on a day

GRANT, JESSE + NELLIE

Jesse + Nellie Grant

BRADY, Photo.   Washington, D.C.

The two younger Grants in Brady's studio.

ULYSS

. . . .

35

D. FREDRICKS & CO., MISS NELLIE GRANT. NEW YORK.

Fred Grant.

his orders had resulted in hideous casualties, perhaps his worst day of the Civil War, Grant could write to Nellie about her pony cart.

The Grants were loyal to their family almost to a fault. When their son Fred was a cadet at West Point (and his father president of the United States), he brought discredit to himself and did serious damage not only to a fellow cadet but also to the aspirations of African Americans generally. Cadet James Smith, an African American from South Carolina who was sponsored by a prominent Northern liberal, David Clark, was being harassed far beyond the bounds of hazing in order to drive him from the military academy—and from becoming an officer in the United States Army. Fred was one of his tormentors. Confronted by his father, in Clark's presence, Fred defiantly said, "well, no damned nigger will ever graduate from West Point."[6] Grant, as president, and one with fairly impressive military credentials, might have successfully

---

6. Quoted in William S. McFeely, *Grant: A Biography* (New York: W. W. Norton, 1981), 376.

contradicted this prophecy, but as a father, and very likely at the insistence of a mother, he did no more than ask for an inquiry into the affair. Despite persevering, Cadet Smith, with an excellent academic record, was deliberately failed in an examination by a professor of philosophy and left West Point; Frederick Dent Grant graduated in 1871, in the presence of his parents, and went on to become a second Major General Grant. We can wonder if his father would have acted more vigorously if his son was not one of the culprits.

How black citizens were to fare in postbellum America was a central question in the Grant administration. As Fred and his father had discovered, it impinged on the family as well. When Grant's war ended, and with it slavery—the Thirteenth Amendment was ratified in December 1865—a great movement of black Americans into Washington, D.C., began. Many new citizens, either war refugees or other freed slaves seeking to put behind them not only working for former owners but also simple rural poverty, moved to the nation's capital, from which so much that was beneficial to them emanated. They not only sought economic opportunity, but also believed the nation's capital would welcome them.

However, even those white Washingtonians who might have had sympathy for the mass of downtrodden black people as long as they were slaves down in the South had second thoughts when those same blacks became the neighbors next door in a crowded expanding capital city. No one lived next door to the White House, but we can imagine that some black citizens with pride in a genteel mien would have wanted to attend a reception given by the general—now president—who had been such a key figure in their emancipation. Receptions in the Grants' day were not simply for celebrities and donors, but for the people.

Julia Grant, recalling her early days as the hostess of the house, wrote: "One day as I sat in the library already dressed for my reception, one of the ushers appeared at the door and, bowing low, said: 'Madam, if any colored people call, are they to be admitted?' I, after a moment's thought, said: 'This is my reception day. Admit all who call.' No colored people called, however, nor did they at any time during General Grant's two terms in office, thus showing themselves modest and not aggressive, and I am sure they, as a race, loved him and fully appreciated all that he had done for them."[7]

7. Julia Grant, *Personal Memoirs*, 175.

To put the most favorable face on this passage, you could take her words as tolerant, if patronizing, but you might wonder what had been the look on Mrs. President Grant's face that day in response to the usher's question. And it is not difficult to imagine her relief that no black Washingtonians called—that day and in all eight years of her receptions. The usher, "bowing low," in the best subservient plantation manner, was almost certainly black. If so, with disgust, he would have spread the word to those who were considering paying a call that they might receive a frosty reception.

Social ostracism was a forerunner of all that was to destroy the bright promise that Reconstruction had seemed to hold for black Americans. Julia Grant's upbringing would not have prepared her to see "dear, devoted servants" as guests at the tea table. Her husband, who eschewed familiarity—I know of no African American confidant—seems to have been comfortable with blacks in businesslike meetings. Julia may have had the black vote in mind when she told the usher to let any colored people in; but her relief when none came suggests her own sensibility. Incidents like this lead me to think that she was not a positive influence on her husband when the vexing questions having to do with race kept rising in all their complexity.

In official matters, President Grant often did the right thing with respect to the four million new citizens. But if he had looked back over his eight years in office, he would have been conscious of the decline of sympathy for the former slaves among a vast majority of Americans. Surely those four million people who counted on him took note. In this matter, there is no evidence that Julia helped him stay the course.

As Julia saw it, her job was not to achieve social justice, but to meet the social responsibilities as mistress of the executive mansion. And meet them she eagerly did. Known in the family as "the Boss," she took command in the White House as well. Her predecessor, Eliza Johnson, had been too unwell to do so; Mary Lincoln had been as ambitious, but also tempestuous; there had been no Mrs. Buchanan—it had been a long time since there had been what might be termed an ideal first lady. Dismayed by what she saw as the shabbiness of the house—it was only four years since Mary Lincoln had spent a good deal of money on fresh furnishings, but fashions had changed—Julia had the house redecorated in what came to be called, derisively, Grant style. (It took Jacqueline Kennedy, as eager as Julia Grant to make over the old place, to get rid of the bland neocolonial decor that descended from the redec-

*Julia Grant redecorated
the White House.*

oration of Theodore Roosevelt's White House. Jackie brought it back to a style of grandeur not dissimilar to that which Julia had achieved.)

Julia Grant was anxious to reign, but despite her protestations of having been "in society" as a girl, her hand was not secure. She masked that insecurity in what an eager Washington, where political ambition was the engine of social life, was quick to pronounce pretentious. Julia seems to have had few close female friends to give her a hand, but one ally for almost the full eight years as first lady was invaluable. With Julia Kean Fish at her side—"she would stand near me"[8]—Julia Dent Grant was firmly anchored socially. Julia Fish, the wife of Hamilton Fish, Grant's secretary of state, was such an undoubted patrician (in a democracy that was supposed not to harbor such) as to be above any of the posturing for position so prevalent among politicians and their wives in Washington. Julia Fish, with nothing to gain, was kind, and

8. Ibid.

Hamilton Fish, the able Secretary of State.

Julia Fish. The photographer has created an honest, beautiful portrait.

Julia Grant was grateful. The Fishes invited the Grants to stay with them after they left the White House and before they left the capital.

Here again Julia's *Memoirs* frustrate: "under [this] hospitable roof we remained for some two weeks, until the birth of Mrs. Sartoris's son Algernon. All of the time was taken up by dinners, luncheons, and parties. We hardly had time to rest."[9] Mrs. Sartoris was her daughter, Nellie, and Algernon her second grandchild, and this tantalizing bit of news is all we are to learn about this familial event from the mother's personally deficient *Personal Memoirs*.

If Ulysses's prose reflects his resolute character, Julia's memoirs

9. Ibid, 196.

reveal her in a false light that is often less flattering than she intended. His *Personal Memoirs* had been a vast commercial success; her work did not find a publisher in her lifetime. John Y. Simon, editor of Grant's papers, published her *Personal Memoirs* for the first time in 1975. The expertly edited book was respectfully received but caused nothing like the acclaim that had accrued to her husband's reminiscences. It provides valuable details of the Grants' story, but, on the whole, they disguise rather than reveal her strengths. In fact, Julia Grant's memoir is a rather sad book. After sharing in her husband's fame for thirty years she, as she recollects her life, still feels she must defend her family's social credentials and stress every slight that she, of course, rose above and every social triumph that was, of course, her due. A reader wonders if she would have written exactly as she did if her husband were still alive. As so many great men's wives do, she became a kind of professional widow, tending the fading light of his fame.

Rereading Julia's memoirs, I asked myself if they disguise what she truly wanted to say. Nineteenth-century writers—and they are not alone in this regard—had great difficulty in talking about the subject that was most compelling to them. Herman Melville wrestled with sexuality in virtually all of his work. Emily Dickinson's richly opaque poetry discloses her sense of the erotic only in sudden flashes of unexpected language. Walt Whitman was the least tongue-tied, but even he wouldn't fully let loose. Richard Burton, the translator of the *Kamasutra* and generally the century's sexual wild man, eager as he was to write about sex, found himself at times floundering in odd locutions. If Burton, who could write about peoples' sexual pursuits, could not quite say what sex meant to him, how can we possibly imagine Julia Dent Grant doing so? I have come to think that the idealized praise of her Alexander the Great's mightiness cloaks a terrible loneliness and a yearning for a very corporeal Ulysses Grant.

Julia Grant is credited with keeping her husband sober. Admirers of the general, those willing to admit to his problem with alcohol, routinely credit her with keeping him from drinking. The implication is that "the Boss" insisted on his abstinence. At least as plausible is the possibility that her presence provided a satisfying alternative to the bottle. It is worth noting that at the time he was reported to have been on a drunken tear, during the Vicksburg campaign, not only was Grant frustrated with the inaction of that wearisome operation, but also Julia was not around. The two were married for nearly forty years and, as far

as I can discern, gave up sharing a double bed only when the alternative was his deathbed.

Julia Dent Grant (*above*) was not only an exemplar of our new understanding of the willingness of the nineteenth century's middle class to enjoy sex. Her sense of herself sexually fits as well a tenet of feminism from a century after her time, that women do not have to be conventionally glamorous to be sexually attractive. There was no photographer, though bent on producing the most flattering of portraits, who could make her pretty. Julia, once she found Ulysses, seems not to have let this bother her—nor did it him. There is, of course, no direct evidence of the nature of Julia's or of the couple's sexual activity. There is only an occasional hint of the sexual dimension of her life. She tells, with seeming innocence, in her *Memoirs* of naming the bedpost Ulysses when she was awaiting his return from the Mexican War, waiting for her marriage.

Over the years of thinking about the two Grants, I have come to realize that their sexual life together was a chief source of their mutual strength. Ulysses's early letters—from Mexico: "Dream of me and tell me of your dreams"[10]—and the romantic cast that hovers over Julia's prose give a suggestion of this. If we can credit what she had so disingenuously obscured, it seems only right that we should indulge her reverie on the White House that she had redecorated from top to bottom. She had triumphed. It was to be the place where she was happiest, where her prince, her "Ulyss," as she always called him, was the physically present master of her house. Julia Dent had at last become the princess of White Haven; she was mistress of the White House. "I love the dear old house. . . . Eight happy years I spent there—so happy! It seems as much like home to me as [was] White Haven."[11]

10. John Y. Simon, ed., *The Papers of Ulysses S. Grant*, 24 vols. (Carbondale: Southern Illinois University Press, 1967–c. 2000), 1:118.
11. Julia Grant, *Personal Memoirs*, 174.

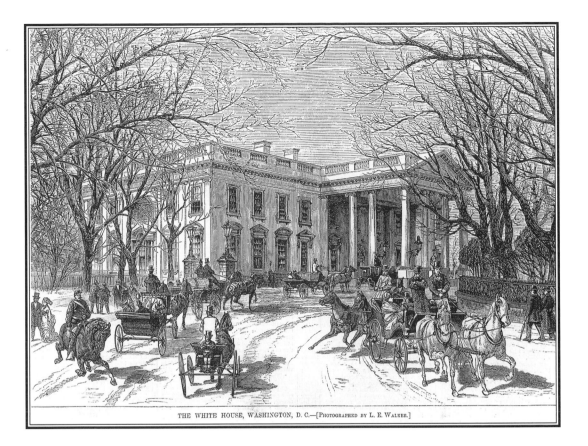

The Grants lived at this address longer than any other.

THE WHITE HOUSE, WASHINGTON, D. C.—[Photographed by L. E. Walker.]

White Haven, Julia's other favorite house.

3

Presenting a
General

Photographers at Work

"Celebrity," as the word is used today, is exactly the wrong one to apply to Ulysses Grant. The very concept corrodes rather than establishes the value of people who have gained the world's attention. Grant's manner was the antithesis of that of so many of today's tinseled celebrities. But the truth of the matter is that Grant was a Civil War hero who was celebrated with many portraits. Preening generals like John Charles Fremont and George B. McClellan sought and found attention in the pictorial journals of the day, *Harper's Weekly* and *Frank Leslie's Illustrated Newspaper*. Grant, without trying, but just by doing his job, caught the attention of editors competing for readers in the midst of the war.

His ordinariness coupled with his effectiveness was the key. Objectively, after the two crucial Union victories in July 1863, at Vicksburg and at Gettysburg, there was no reason why General George Gordon Meade, who stopped Lee's invasion of Pennsylvania, should not have been the hero who caught the public's eye. Instead, it was General

Grant, whose long campaign resulted in the taking of the stronghold on the Mississippi, who did. In part this was because the press, as a molder of public opinion, had never cottoned to the arrogant Philadelphian who battled reporters. At a point in 1862 when Grant was getting poor press, rather than protesting he simply confided in Julia: "I hope the paper will let me alone in the future. . . . I do not look much at the papers now consequently save myself much uncomfortable feeling."[1] He let the reporters do their job while he did his.

Other generals were known for their exploits and careers before the Civil War. Grant, in contrast, was an unknown clerk in a harness store when the war began. He did not stay obscure for long. He once enigmatically said, "War is progressive"; there can be no doubt that his rise in the ranks during the Civil War showed swift progress. Grant began the war a colonel, and he did not achieve that rank as quickly as he thought he deserved. Other West Point men who had left the army were soon called back into service to lead the huge untrained armies that the governors provided to Abraham Lincoln immediately after Fort Sumter was fired on and the Civil War began.

Grant, on the other hand, had to prove his worth. Immediately on the call of Illinois men, he went to Springfield to drill recruits and hope for his commission. It was, it seemed to him, so slow in coming that he thought of giving it all up and going back to Galena. His record in the peacetime army, clouded by his drinking (which gossip had undoubtedly embellished), caused him to be bypassed. Grant's ability (and a regimental colonel's incompetence) combined with a push from his hometown congressman did the trick. Late in June 1861, Grant became colonel of the Illinois Twenty-third Regiment.

Aroused and self-confident, he led his men into a Missouri that was engaged in its own civil war over where the state's loyalty lay. Grant's job was to assist in the defeat of the armed effort to hold Missouri for the Confederacy. It was here that he fought his first Civil War battle. On July 16, 1861, President Lincoln appointed twenty-six men to the rank of brigadier general, Grant among them. The army needed leaders, and a colonel who had fought well in Missouri now had a record worthy of promotion. The press did not yet single him out. The only formal portrait of Grant taken before the war of which I am aware is the one that

---

1. U. S. Grant to Julia Grant, April 25, 1862, in Simon, ed., *Papers of Ulysses S. Grant*, 5:72.

was taken just after he received his commission as second lieutenant upon leaving West Point. There is none of the new brigadier general. Only when he became famous did the oak tree under which he is said to have received his commission to that rank also gain recognition.

Moving to Cairo, at the juncture of the Ohio and Mississippi Rivers, he led his troops into Kentucky to take Fort Henry, on the Tennessee River, which guarded access to the Confederacy. Actually, not the army but Union gunboats accomplished that surrender. Grant then moved overland to Fort Donelson, similarly guarding access to Tennessee, on the Cumberland River. On February 16, 1862, Grant's men won that

Copyrighted, 1898, by H. C. Townsend.

THE GRANT OAK,
AT IRONTON, MO.,
UNDERNEATH WHICH
COL. ULYSSES S. GRANT
RECEIVED HIS COMMISSION AS
BRIGADIER GENERAL.
ON IRON MOUNTAIN ROUTE.

PHOTO BY
TER B. TOWNSEND 1892.

HARPER'S WEEKLY.

JOURNAL OF CIVILIZATION.

Vol. VI.—No. 271.] NEW YORK, SATURDAY, MARCH 8, 1862. [SINGLE COPIES SIX CENTS. $2 50 PER YEAR IN ADVANCE.

Entered according to Act of Congress, in the Year 1862, by Harper & Brothers, in the Clerk's Office of the District Court for the Southern District of New York.

MAJOR-GENERAL ULYSSES S. GRANT, U.S.A., THE HERO OF FORT DONELSON.—FROM A PHOTOGRAPH.—[SEE PAGE 151.]

battle. The Union had a much needed victory and Lincoln had a fighting general. The harness store clerk of a year earlier was promoted and rewarded with the equivalent of having his picture on the cover of this week's *Time*. *Harper's Weekly* featured on its first page a picture of the recently promoted "Major General Ulysses S. Grant, U.S.A. The Hero of Fort Donelson."

The only problem is that it is not a picture of Grant. *Harper's*, eager to feature the army's first hero, rushed to print. In 1862, it was

not possible to reproduce a photograph in print. The method was for a steel engraver to work from a photograph, in this case, a photograph of another general thought, I suppose, to look like Grant. You can only think that the editors figured that no one would know the difference.

A photograph (*above*) from, I suspect, the same photographer's studio has long fascinated me. At first glance it is simply the worst picture of Grant ever taken. The uniform is pretentious, the hat askew, and he appears to be have a double beard, one below and behind the other. On closer inspection, I suspect that some enterprising photographer obtained a perfectly nice photograph of Grant (from where, I don't know) with his beard and pasted it on top of another photograph of a long-bearded, uniformed general, after cutting out that officer's face. Then he took a third glass-plate negative, this time of his cut-and-paste amalgam. (Historians of photography, taking up the quest, have discovered a half-dozen versions of this doctored picture. If photography recently has been accused of being an instrument used to corrupt paintings, it is worth noting that it is not itself an art form of strict purity.)

A clue that this is what is going on in this photograph is the uniform and the pose. It was customary to insert the hand between the buttons of your jacket to hold it steady during long exposures, but the Napoleonic hand inserted well into the uniform's jacket, the better to scratch his belly, was not Grant's style. (He had no use for Napoleon and would not have aped him.) Neither does the body seem right—it does not appear to be Grant's chunky torso—nor was Grant one to adorn himself with epaulettes.

The man himself appears in this superior portrait of Major General Grant (*opposite*), a study taken by Matthew Brady or one of his staff of superb portraitists. The photographer has caught a characteristically thoughtful Grant after winning the battle of Shiloh. There, on the Tennessee River, he had met a large Confederate force, which only retreated after fierce fighting, a near defeat of the Union troops, and terrible casualties. It was there that Grant came to realize that the war would be a long one, won only when the defiant South was crushed.

Grant held the rank of major general for two momentous years, during which he led the long and finally successful capture of Vicksburg in July 1863, establishing Union control of the Mississippi River. Recognized now as a masterful general, he was, that fall, ordered to the southeast corner of Tennessee to break the siege of Union forces at Chattanooga. Reassembling the armies of the western theater of the war, he succeeded in a major defeat of the Confederate army. Here was a general able to take command and act. President Lincoln had his general.

On March 9, 1864, Grant was appointed lieutenant general. Before him, only George Washington had held the rank, then the highest in the army. With his new post, Grant was put in command of all the Union armies. *Harper's* rival, *Frank Leslie's Illustrated Newspaper* celebrated the occasion in its March 19 edition with a fanciful image of

Major General Ulysses S. Grant.

Grant. He was now *the* Union general, and the paper celebrated him as such. *Leslie's* was a full-sized newspaper; a heroic Grant mounted triumphantly on a mighty steed was printed sideways across both pages of the centerfold. As it was virtually a poster, I suspect admiring young boys tacked it up on a good many Northern bedroom walls.

Closer to the real Grant is the familiar photograph (*opposite, top*) taken outside his headquarters at City Point, Virginia, later in the war. This, my favorite picture of Grant, suggests both the relaxed confi-

dence of a general commanding a vast, virtually conti-
nent-wide army in a vast war and the irony that so
pleasant and simple-appearing a person was that commander. It is interesting to compare the photograph
taken by one of the talented Matthew Brady group
with the engraving of it that appeared in *Harper's*.
(*right*). Grant is similarly at home in the photograph of
him with his horse (page 56). The commanding hero

on horseback of the *Leslie's* centerfold is, here, a small man at ease, his hand resting gently on the shoulder of his horse. The animal seems equally comfortable with the general. There is no picture of Grant on horseback leading his army into battle so, again, in the photograph on page 57, a photographer went to work, applying considerable poetic—or cut-and-paste—license.

Photographers were not the only artists that recognized Grant as a horseman. C. W. Reed, artist of the Civil War, drew an energetic Grant, hunched over in the saddle, cigar in his mouth (page 58, *top*). Less dashing, but closer to the man, is the imagining of a pensive general

A cut-and paste General Grant.

astride a horse (page 59) done in the twentieth century by perhaps our greatest illustrator, N. C. Wyeth. When Grant came to be memorialized in stone in the twentieth century, an equestrian statue was called for. Daniel Chester French took on Grant. Rather than a "general on horse-back," with Grant in heroic pose, French has given us a compact little man on a horse. Another sculptor, Edward Clark Potter, a master of animal figures, gave Grant a horse less restrained than its rider. And so, Grant sternly confronts Philadelphians mounted on his favorite horse, his famous Cincinnati (page 58, *bottom*).

In 1902, Henry Merwin Shrady (his father had been Grant's last

C. W. Reed's drawing of Grant and Cincinnati, characteristically in motion.

In Philadelphia, Grant and his horse are uncharacteristically sedate.

N. C. Wyeth, the great illustrator, has Grant just right.

physician) was given the commission for the impressive Grant monument at the base of the capitol in Washington, perhaps the most heroic of the statuary commemorating the general. On one side of the vast piece, completed in 1927, the horses plunge rather than pull; the gun carriage becomes a chariot of war (*below*). In the center of it all is Grant splendidly on horseback (*opposite*).

In a bas-relief at the foot of the Grant statue, determined infantrymen, each a distinct person, thrust themselves into battle. These Civil War soldiers are all white. By the twentieth century, sculptors, like so many of their compatriots, had forgotten that the Civil War was not simply a white man's war. In 1897, the sculptor Augustus Saint-Gaudens had remembered, as had Grant, that Civil War soldiers were not all of one hue. On what is perhaps our finest urban monument, Boston's *Shaw*

A towering equestrian Grant.

Augustus Saint-Gaudens's individualized men of
the Massachusetts Fifty-fourth.

Memorial, Augustus Saint-Gaudens portrayed the white Robert Gould Shaw leading men of the Massachusetts Fifty-fourth, the first black regiment to be recruited in the North, into battle. This sculptor's soldiers, equally as determined as Shrady's, are fully realized portraits of black men, many of whom, with their colonel, were to fall at Fort Wagner.

None of these grand ceremonial statements portrays Grant as fully as do the best of the Brady pictures. Even in a formal full-figured portrait (*opposite*), Grant defies celebrity. Captured for posterity as the victorious general in command, Grant, in his face, bears a trace of his haunting simplicity.

A fit General Grant.

376

THE SIEGE OF PETERSBURG—BURYING THE DEAD BEFORE CEMETERY HILL UNDER A FLAG OF TRUCE, AFTER THE REPULSE OF THE NINTH ARMY CORPS.—FROM A SKETCH BY E. F. MULLEN.

4

"No Pen Portray"

Grant and the Meaning of War

I have written about the Civil War, but I cannot claim to have written about war. Both are inevitably with us when we look at Ulysses S. Grant. If he had not been the warrior he became, we would never have heard of him. The subject of his *Personal Memoirs of U. S. Grant* is the Civil War, but even there he has not gotten to its core. He tells vividly of the Mexican War and at greater length of the Civil War. Military historians admit him as a master of their genre. Historians of both wars still go to his narratives as they write their own studies. But although Grant's admirable accounts of two American wars tell the story well, what they do not do is tell how he or any of his men, or the civilians in their way, experienced battle.

Personal Memoirs leaves us with the same quandary about the nature of war that so much military history does. It sometimes feels that the dispassionate accounts of history's wars are the last place to go to know what war is. Why is it that so many general readers, as well as more than a few historians, come away from formal studies of a war with a sense that the central point has been missed? The details of campaigns and battles, their effect on the political landscape, the pileup of statistics, however chilling, do not get to war's brutal essence.

Instead, we turn to other sources to try to grasp a thread of the reality of war. Many of us go first to the fiction of Pat Barker and Ian McEwan and Tim O'Brien to feel the texture of war rather than to the shelves of scholarly histories of World Wars I and II and the Vietnam War. There is more, somehow, in the mordant minutiae of Ambrose Bierce than in the full narrative of Ken Burns's documentary film *The Civil War*, rich with color and lush with music.

I claim no true reality for the following pictures—photographs or their reproduction for the press as engravings—that were among the thousands of images available from 1861 to 1865 and from which people far from the battlefield tried to make sense of the war. Families at

Artists can make war heroic.

home had these and their fearful imaginings of what their men were experiencing. *Harper's Illustrated Weekly* and *Frank Leslie's Illustrated Newspaper* were the most famous providers of the thousands of pictures of the Civil War. People in the North learned of the war from many verbal sources: other newspapers, letters home from the front, and endless rumors. But it was the illustrations that enabled them to build a visual image of Grant in the Civil War.

Most readers met Grant first in February 1862, after his victory at Fort Donelson. In this, the North's first victory, he bested his Confederate foe, his old friend Simon Bolivar Buckner. Lincoln had in Grant a general who could fight—and win. The Union cause had a hero— and one newspaper carried far too optimistic an evaluation of the result

Both friend and foe.

HARPER'S WEEKLY.

SATURDAY, MARCH 1, 1862.

THE BEGINNING OF THE END.

THE capture of Fort Donelson, with 15,000 men, including both the Generals Buckner and Bushrod Johnston, is probably the culminating point in the struggle between the United States Government and the malcontents. At the hour we write General Buell, with 80,000 men, is pressing upon the Cumberland River; while General Grant, with 50,000, and Flag-officer Foote, with his gun-boat and mortar fleet, are ascending the same stream from the bend at Dover. Rumor states that the remnant of the garrison of Fort Donelson, with part of the Bowling Green army, have taken refuge at Clarksville, and seem disposed to make a stand there. If they do, they will inevitably share the fate of the army which has just surrendered. The events of the past week have rendered us indisputable masters of the Cumberland and Tennessee rivers, of Nashville and all Northern Tennessee, and of the Virginia and Tennessee Railroad. Wherever we meet the enemy we shall be three to one, and by far superior to them in equipments, commissariat, clothing, transportation, and arms.

The fate of Columbus, Memphis, and consequently New Orleans, is now sealed. It is hardly probable that the right reverend rebel Leonidas Polk will wait to be caught in the trap he has built for himself at Columbus. If he does, we shall by-and-by take him and all his force without firing a gun. If he evacuates his present post, the rebels themselves admit that they can not defend any other point on the Mississippi. One Union army of enormous strength will advance on Memphis from Nashville, while another Union army under Halleck's generals will drive Price before them through Arkansas, and both will meet on the Mississippi in time to co-operate with Flag-officer Foote's gun-boat and mortar-fleet. Unless some unforeseen accident occurs the whole Mississippi will be ours, from the Gulf to Cairo, by 15th March.

Meanwhile, Burnside is cutting off the retreat of the Virginia army through North Carolina, and making ready to take Norfolk. When he was at the mouth of the Roanoke the people of Weldon fled from their houses. Norfolk should be in our possession as soon as Memphis.

Simultaneously, Dupont and Sherman are moving against Savannah, and Commodore Porter's fleet is on the way to Mobile and New Orleans.

Against such a combination of forces working together on such a plan, how long can the rebellion last?

"NO PEN
PORTRAY"
. . . .

of the battle (*left*). Donelson would soon be dwarfed by other far more terrible battles. The first of these for Grant came that April at Shiloh. Moving south along the Tennessee River to Pittsburg Landing, his army encountered the major Confederate force advancing to meet them. The Union force was driven back with terrible losses on the first day. Characteristically, Grant did not back off, but, on the second day, attacked, and the rebels retreated.

Grant's next great campaign was the long struggle to take control of the whole stretch of the Mississippi River. A famous Currier and Ives print depicts, in lurid detail, the Union navy gunboats running the gauntlet of Confederate fire from Vicksburg (*opposite, top*). After Grant succeeded in taking the city and, with it, the command of the river, in July 1863, he became a great hero in the North. Lincoln sent Secretary of War Edward Stanton to give Grant command of all the Union armies in the west and ordered him to rescue the bottled-up Union force at Chattanooga. *Harper's* let its readers see the miserably tough and unspectacular work of preparing for battle (*opposite, bottom*). It was on just such a trail that Grant himself, with a wounded leg, rode his horse over the mountain into Chattanooga to take command and order up the supplies and troops that successfully battled to break the siege and take control of southeastern Tennessee.

Now President Lincoln and members of Congress thought they had the general who could command not the armies of one vast theater of war in the west, but those of the whole Union army, west and east—and press on until the South was crushed. Grant was named lieutenant general and moved his command to Virginia. For two years, other Union generals in the east had been turned back each time they had tried to take Richmond. Grant would not turn back. He pushed his army through the horror of the Wilderness campaign and, at Cold Harbor, tried to take the Confederate capital with a frontal assault. In *Leslie's* of 1864 is a picture of that terrible battle of Cold Harbor (page 70), one of only two battles—the other was outside Vicksburg—that Grant later regretted having fought. The picture purports to show "the repulse of Lee's attack on General Smith," while in truth things were

DESIGNED BY CURRIER & IVES.   Entered according to act of Congress in the year 1863, by Currier & Ives in the Clerk's Office of the District Court of the United States for the Southern District of New York.   152 NASSAU ST. N.Y.

TUSCUMBIA.   HENRY CLAY, FOREST QUEEN, SILVER WAVE, CARANDELET, PITTSBURG, MOUND CITY,   LOUISVILLE.   LAFAYETTE & GEN! PRICE.   FLAG SHIP BENTON.

ADMIRAL PORTER'S FLEET RUNNING THE REBEL BLOCKADE OF THE MISSISSIPPI AT VICKSBURG, APRIL 16TH 1863.

At half past ten P.M. the boats left their moorings & steamed down the river, the Benton, Admiral Porter, taking the lead _____ as they approached the point opposite the town, a terrible and concentrated fire of the centre, upper and lower batteries, both water and bluff, was directed upon the channel, which here ran within one hundred yards of the shore. At the same moment immense fire rafts, floats of turpentine and other combustible materials were set ablaze. In the face of all this fire, the boats made their way with but little loss except the transport Henry Clay which was set on fire and burnt.

HARPER'S WEEKLY.

NOVEMBER 21, 1863.

THE WAR IN EAST TENNESSEE—DRAWING ARTILLERY THROUGH THE MOUNTAINS.—[SEE PAGE 742.]

GRANT'S CAMPAIGN IN VIRGINIA—REPULSE OF LEE'S NIGHT ATTACK ON SMITH'S BRIGADE, ARMY OF THE POTOMAC, FRIDAY, JUNE 3.—From a Sketch by our Special Artist, Edwin Forbes.—See Page 231.

Cold Harbor, Virginia.

going very wrong for Smith, for Grant, and for both generals' men. Whatever impression readers of *Leslie's* were left with, it could not have encompassed the agony of the wounded men dying in the June sun in Virginia.

Moving south of Richmond, Grant laid siege to Petersburg. His command post was farther east, at City Point. There he commanded all the vastly spread Union armies in their victorious course. Finally, his own army broke the siege of Petersburg and at Appomattox achieved the Confederate surrender that ended the war.

This cursory pictorial rundown of Grant's progress through the war suggests how people at home were led by the press to envision the drama of the campaigns and his eventual triumph. Similar images, amassed and enhanced by present-day technology, depict, in turn, how we today are

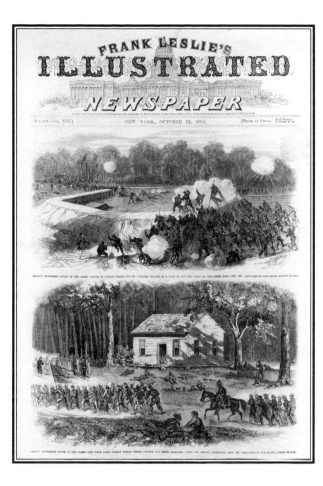

How those at home saw
the war.

Petersburg, Virginia.

invited to remember it. I am not sure how much even the most graphic photographs tell us—nor, finally, any narrative. James M. McPherson, the leading historian of the American Civil War, has written a careful study of the battle of Antietam, with details of the battle and a careful analysis of its determining role in the outcome of the war. Tucked away in his careful, dispassionate account is a paragraph of his finest prose:

"Night fell on a scene of horror beyond imagining: 2,108 Union dead and estimates ranging from 1,546 to 2,700 Confederate dead on the battlefield; 9,549 Union wounded and estimates of 7,752 to 9,024 Confederate wounded. Of the wounded on both sides, at least 2,000 would die of their wounds. The detritus of battle lay thickly on the field: smashed weapons and gun carriages, dead horses, scraps of bloody clothing, discarded knapsacks and blanket rolls, and the smell of rotting corpses, vomit, and excrement."[1]

Then, at the paragraph's close, McPherson adds a sentence that exposes the irony of even so fine a passage: " 'No tongue can tell, no mind can conceive, no pen portray the horrible sights I witnessed' as the sun rose next morning, a Pennsylvania soldier wrote in his diary."[2]

And, he might have added, no camera. A famous picture by Alexander Gardner of one of the thousands of corpses left on the battlefield of Antietam (*opposite*) was shown in Brady's spacious, fashionable New York gallery. Hundreds of visitors found their eyes both averted from and drawn to the gruesome image and came nearer war's reality. But the surviving soldier who had not words for the battle that killed the man would have faulted their grasp on war's horror. Somehow, the very fact that the corpse was dragged into place—posed for the most effective shot—speaks to even the camera's inability to tell fully of war. And certainly, the album of curiously passive and peaceful pictures of the war by that same Alexander Gardner (pages 74–75) stand in almost obscene contrast to what he had seen at Antietam.

Our memory of the war is full of these contradictory images that for so many Americans seem to feed rather than discourage a seemingly endless fascination with the Civil War. This urge not to let go of that war is most prominent among the descendants of the men who lost the war. But what, long after, did Grant remember? The nation was the

1. James M. McPherson, *Crossroads of Freedom: Antietam* (New York: Oxford University Press, 2002), 129.
2. Ibid.

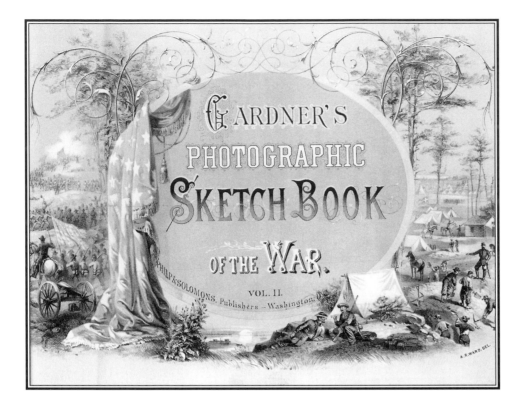

Creating a memory of war.

Gardner shows a quiet moment.

Away from battle.

beneficiary of his determination and relentless pursuit of victory in the war that ended slavery, and by ending slavery gave the war its justification. (That his nation, so proud of its political structure, had not been able to find a method other than war to do that essential job was not his fault.) Was there for Grant any personal toll as there so surely was on the dead, and on the survivors maimed physically and psychologically?

If there was such a price, there is no evidence of it; he would seem to have insulated himself from such emotions. Or at least, when talking of war, to have either successfully sublimated such feelings or, possibly, found them too terrible to confront and discuss. Somewhat to the amazement of John Russell Young, the reporter who accompanied the general on his 1877–79 trip around the world, Grant did, on shipboard, reminisce about the Civil War. His assessments were remarkably clear-sighted and direct. What enabled him to accomplish what he did in the Civil War was that he was in good shape: "A successful general needs health and youth and energy. . . . When I was in the army I had a physique that could stand anything. Whether I slept on the ground or in a tent, whether I slept one hour or ten . . . whether I had one meal or three, or none, made no difference. I could lie down and sleep in the rain," as he did after the first disastrous day at Shiloh.[3] He might have added that the ability simply to sleep was crucial. He does not allude to the rare, but fierce, migraines that at moments of great stress threatened to incapacitate him.

Approaching as closely as he ever did to a theory of war, he told Young, "War is progressive, because all the instruments and elements of war are progressive."[4] "Progressive" is always a tricky word and an odd one to choose for war. I have come to think that he is telling us that war is not a single battle, or a single factor of any kind, but rather the sum of many that must be played out sequentially and in full. He saw the Civil War as a terrible, difficult, and calmly exhilarating story with a beginning, one chock-full of events—numerous, but comprehensible—and an ending. For the Union the story had its men, more numerous than those of the enemy; its leaders, most significantly Abraham Lincoln; and its moral, the sanctity of the Union, and, as the war progressed, the freeing of the slaves.

3. Quoted in Young, *Around the World*, 2:353.
4. Ibid.

War for Grant was not simply a matter of forces beyond man's control. He was thoughtful in his assessments of his fellow generals and how they did or did not accept responsibility. "I do not believe in luck in war," he told Young, "any more than in luck in business. Luck is a small matter, may effect a battle or a movement, but not a campaign or career."[5] Grant apparently did not credit his years at West Point as luck—he disliked the place so much—but would we ever have heard of him if his father hadn't sent him there? Instead of an anonymous private (or a stay-at-home civilian, as I have always been), Grant was an officer, and he must have realized that that had mattered. But, if luck played a part in his gaining the responsibility he had in the war, he never counted on it during a campaign; he credited it for neither success nor failure.

Grant ticked off the things that had defeated other generals— "Some . . . like Hooker at Chancellorsville, because when they won a victory they lost their heads, and did not know what to do with it."[6] Other generals failed to have his visual sense of what they were doing as a commander. McClellan, for example, among his other quirks, was obsessed with numbers as he contemplated a coming battle or an ongoing campaign. Grant was, of course, mindful of what he could deduce of the size of his opponent's force in relation to his own, but that was simply one factor of many as he visualized what lay ahead.

Grant's visual sense was a trait that was crucial to his success as a general. He saw the lay of the land. As he traveled the globe, he often seemed not to be taking in the scenery, but visualizing what it would have been like to fight in the terrain he was looking at. "Compare," he said to Young, "the invasion of France by the Germans [in the Franco-Prussian War of 1870] with the invasion of the South. The Germans moved from town to town, every town being a base of supply. They had no bridges to build. They had no corduroy roads to make, and I question if a corduroy road was made in the whole campaign."[7]

Of all the courses that Grant took at West Point the one he liked best was his drawing class with Robert Weir (page 78). Contrary to

---

5. Ibid.
6. Ibid., 352.
7. Ibid.

An older Robert Walker Weir. He was in his late thirties when Grant studied with him.

what might be thought of such a course in relation to those more conventionally military, it may have been the one that best equipped him to fight. Reminiscing, Grant told Young, "The only eyes a general can trust are his own. He must be able to see and know the country, the streams, the passes, the hills. You look on a map and you see a pass in Switzerland. You know there is such a pass, but in a military sense you know nothing."[8] In other words, Grant, as he traveled, saw a rugged path through formidable mountains and knew that the act of struggling through that terrain would be very different from either reading a map of the area or drawing a landscape, as he had done twenty years earlier in school. In command of all the Union armies, Grant was also

8. Ibid.

able "to see and know,"—even visualize—the entire terrain of the more than ten-state battleground of a war that covered a third of the continental United States.

There was no moving of toy soldiers on a map in Grant's war-making. Nor was he trusting of any dogma: "Some of our generals failed because they worked out everything by rule. They knew what Frederick [the Great] did at one place, what Napoleon at another. They were always thinking about what Napoleon would do. Unfortunately for their plans, the rebels would be thinking about something else."[9] Grant fought by no rule. He saw the lay of the land as he went into battle, saw it the morning after a battle, and faced up to the totally unpredictable circumstances he now had to face. Nothing happened as planned, everything changed.

We ought not forget that this immense accomplishment was achieved only through a war filled with nights like that experienced by the soldier on the field at Antietam. Grant saw scenes of equal horror on the battlefield. How did he react? You search in vain through the general's wartime letters as well as his *Memoirs* for his emotional reaction to war. Of one thing I am certain; he was never in the grasp of any mythical concept of war's goodness. He would never have said: "Compared to war all forms of human endeavor shrink to insignificance. God, I do love it so."[10] But the fact remains that Grant was aroused by war, as he was not by any peacetime endeavor, including his presidency. His was not the arousal of blatant sexuality, of phallic impulse; rather it was for him as it is in Chris Hedges's searing meditation on war, *War Is a Force That Gives Us Meaning*.[11] Hedges looks war squarely in the face and finds it to be both terrible and exhilarating. So did Grant.

Grant, in letters in the 1840s, was amazingly perceptive in his analysis of how President James K. Polk, safely in the White House, maneuvered to get the United States into war with Mexico by skillfully outwitting the opponents of war. Forty years later he had not changed his mind: "to this day [I] regard the war . . . as one of the most unjust

9. Ibid., 355.

10. This famous line, widely attributed to George S. Patton, appears in numerous anthologies of quotations, but none give a citation. This time the bellicose general may have been falsely accused.

11. Chris Hedges, *War Is a Force That Gives Us Meaning* (New York: PublicAffairs, 2002).

ever waged by a stronger against a weaker nation."[12] And yet, fighting in that war, he was energized in a way that he would not be again until the Civil War. He saw the Civil War in a different light than he had the Mexican War. For one thing, in Mexico he was sensitive to the plight of the peasants caught between two marauding armies. In the Civil War he seems to have disciplined himself not to dwell on the civilians, black and white, that inevitably were made refugees. The saving of the Union and the ending of slavery (he came to see these as one and the same thing) made that a war that had to be. As a general he could lead his men into terrible battles with unrelenting force until the war was won.

This still begs the question of how he could bring that force to bear, seeing as he did the terrors he had led his men into. You might say he was too busy fighting the war to think about it. Certainly there were unconscious strategies that enabled him not to be paralyzed by the carnage. One was his astonishing ability to compartmentalize his feelings. On the evening of a day when he had condemned his men to the most terrible of nights, at Cold Harbor in July 1864, Grant could write affectionately to his daughter, Nellie, about her pony cart.

Grant steeled himself against the horrors he sent his men into, but he would not have been other than baffled and disgusted with a Theodore Roosevelt for his admiration of war as imbuing manly virtue. Nor was there in Grant the icy disdain of a Douglas Haig, the British commander in World War I who, safely well behind the lines and deafened to reality, could send his men out of the trenches into the roar of almost certain death. It may have been that the screams and moans of his men, which Grant was close enough to hear, could be borne only with thoughts of a daughter safely removed from the atrocity of the sound. She would be spared the memory, as he was not.

Grant must have had memories, rather than simply a remarkable recall of events. He experienced the war with his men right there on the ground, the bloody ground. His consciousness of what he had been through was so complete that it seems impossible that his unconscious could have escaped unscathed. Something more than the cool recollec-

12. U. S. Grant, *Personal Memoirs*, 1:53.

tion of happenings must have lingered. Long after the war, did memories, pale and terrible, but not unlike the immediate vivid horror experienced by the Pennsylvania soldier that night at Antietam, haunt Grant's nights? Were they of war's reality—a reality that even his pen could not portray?

⤛ 5 ⤜

Havens and Houses

The Peripatetic Grants

At Christmas dinner on board the *Vandalia* in 1877 (page 84, *top*), Julia declared that she was happy, that she felt "at home." She was in the Mediterranean and ten months away from America—and would be away for another two years. Perhaps she was bravely covering her homesickness, her longing for a familiar hearth and table on Christmas Day, but it is possible that her remark was genuine. From the time they left their childhood homes—Ulysses off to West Point and Julia when they married, the couple had seldom had more than a temporary place to call their own. Their eight years in the White House were the longest they called one address theirs.

Julia grew up at White Haven, outside St. Louis, Missouri (page 84, *bottom*). Ulysses was born in a lovely spot within sight of the Ohio River, in Point Pleasant, Ohio (page 85, *top*). When Ulysses was only eighteen months old, the Grant family moved inland to Georgetown, Ohio (page 85, *bottom*). The house there was more securely middle

Christmas on board ship. A rare rendering of Grant with glass in hand.

White Haven, where Julia once celebrated holidays.

Grant was born in Point Pleasant, a lovely spot on the Ohio River.

Georgetown. The house Grant grew up in, with the hated tannery across the street.

Grant's school.

class than the earlier one, and it had the drawback that Grant's father, Jesse, had the smelly, noisy, tannery, which the boy hated, just across the street. But it was in Georgetown that the boy went to school (*above*)— and began his lifelong love affair with horses.

For four years, 1840–43—weary years, he tells us—Grant had as his residence the United States Military Academy at West Point. His first posting after graduation was Jefferson Barracks, outside St. Louis and close, fortunately, to White Haven and Julia. When President James Polk was building up for a war with Mexico, Grant was assigned to a post in Louisiana and then was moved to Texas's Gulf Coast. When the Mexican War began, Grant served first with General Zachary Taylor and then under General Winfield Scott, with whom he entered Mexico City.

West Point, a romantic view.

Corpus Christi, Texas, on the way to the Mexican War.

After the war, Julia and Ulysses were married; their first peacetime army house was in Detroit. (Above, it is decked in mourning at the time of Grant's death.) Next, they were at Madison Barracks, north of the Adirondack Mountains in far upstate New York. Ulysses proudly bought furniture for their quarters, which soon housed their first child. But they were shortly uprooted. He was ordered to a post in the Pacific

Fort Vancouver.

Northwest and, pregnant with their second son, Julia went to stay with her family. Lonely apart from her, Ulysses was stationed first at Fort Vancouver, on the Columbia River in what is now the state of Oregon, and later at Fort Humboldt, in northern California.

After leaving the army, on land borrowed from his father-in-law, to be sure, Grant came as close as he ever was to having his own place, his own home. He cleared the land, hoed potatoes, and felled the timbers he used to build his house. He called it Hardscrabble; the name fit the coarse simplicity of the sturdy building. He took pride in his accomplishment, but once again he was bested. The potatoes rotted, and Julia hated the frontier-cabin look of the house, so in contrast to her family's nearby White Haven. When farming and later bill collecting in Missouri did not work out, Grant had to turn to his father for a job.

In 1860, the Grants moved to Galena, Illinois, where Ulysses worked in the family harness shop. Ulysses Grant walked to work using a steep flight of stairs down to the town and climbed back when the shop closed for the day. Neighbors told of how weary he looked at the end of each dull day. In the pleasant house high on the bluff (*page 92*) overlooking the business section of town there was the restoring energy of the family: Fred, ten, Buck, eight, Nellie, five, and two-year-old

Grant was proud of Hardscrabble. Julia hated the place.

Galena, Illinois. The harness shop where Grant worked is down the block.

Jesse. This domesticity lasted only a matter of months before Ulysses went off to war. The house (*opposite*) that the proud citizens of Galena built for their local hero after the war was never truly the Grants' home in the sense that the earlier one had been. They spent only a rare few days in it.

During the war, Julia was with Ulysses in his headquarters as often as possible. Her presence, remarkably frequent, was a sustaining force for her warrior husband. At the war's end, they were in a house almost as simple as Hardscrabble. This was the surprisingly domestic head-quarters of the commander of the whole of the armies of the United States, at City Point, Virginia. Although Grant—and surely Julia—was to hanker for more in the way of a house, it was here that Ulysses Grant

The comfortable house where the Grants lived when the Civil War began.

THE PRESENT RESIDENCE OF LIEUTENANT-GENERAL U. S. GRANT, GALENA.

Grant did come back "home" to await being elected president.

was most himself. In the photograph below, Jesse, their youngest child, is with his parents.

The war over, the family moved to Washington, D.C. After leaving a house in Georgetown, they moved a bit nearer what politicians, if not Grant, saw as the center of things—into the White House. Opposite (*top*), the young Grant children are off to school. The family spent summers on the Jersey Shore at Long Branch in a cottage that was the prettiest place in which they ever lived. When their eight years in the White House were up and their two and a half years of touring the

Grant, Jesse, and Julia at City Point, Virginia.

PRESIDENT GRANT'S COTTAGE AT LONG BRANCH.—[Phot. by E. W. Pach.]

world were over, they moved into a fine house at 3 East Sixty-sixth Street in New York City (*below*).

Whatever solidity the house represented at first, it was there that Grant had to endure first the ignominy of the failure of yet another business and then the constant scrutiny of the press reporting exhaustively on the progress of his dying. To get Ulysses away from the heat

of the city and, not incidently, to enhance their investment in resort real estate, friends arranged for the Grant family to spend the summer of 1885 on Mt. McGregor, outside Saratoga Springs, New York. In the photograph above, the trees, grown since the Grants' day, fill and darken the clearing in which the pleasant summer cottage stood.

The family gathered to be with Grant and, despite the heat, dressed to the nines for a picture on the porch (page 98). Left to right, they are Ulysses, Jr. "Buck"; Julia; Nellie; Fred's daughter, Julia; Grant; Fred's son, Ulysses S. Grant, III; Fred's wife, Ida; Fred; Jesse's daughter, Nellie; Jesse's wife, Elizabeth; and Jesse. Not surprisingly, this is scarcely a casual summer vacation picture. The family, though not, of course, in mourning clothes, seems almost posed for a mourning picture. The

Buck, Julia, Nellie, Julia (Fred's daughter), Grant, Ulysses S. Grant III (Fred's son), Ida (Fred's wife), Fred, Nellie (Jesse's daughter), Elizabeth (Jesse's wife), and Jesse.

man for whom they will soon grieve, with a high silk hat replacing the protective cap his illness called for and a white scarf at his neck to comfort the cancerous throat that later that summer would kill him, makes no pretense of cheer.

In many ways it had been a peripatetic life for the rather ordinary, grown-a-bit-stout American couple. But there was to be nothing ordinary, certainly nothing private, about their final resting place. It defied the simplicity that Ulysses S. Grant had always presented to the world. When the general died, in 1885, he was buried first in a temporary grave in a New York City public park. Then, in 1897, his remains were moved into the grandest tomb of any of our presidents, high on the then remote Upper West Side of the city. When she died, in 1902, Julia joined Ulysses there. George Washington's remains could lie in the ground of a farm he loved. Ulysses Grant had no soil he could call his own to receive him. In chilly magnificence, two vast bronze sarcophagi lie side by side in the open stone crypt under the too-splendid rotunda of Grant's Tomb.

6

Waifs Abroad

Around the World with General Grant

Presidents of the United States have not done particularly well with retirement. John Quincy Adams's return to the House of Representatives to do battle against slavery and Jimmy Carter's crusade for justice around the world are splendid exceptions. None has matched Ulysses and Julia Grant's approach to the problem, taking a two-and-a-half-year-long trip around the world. As such enterprises go it was often close to being comic, even suggesting a musical comedy, particularly as attested to by the many steel engravings that illustrate the two-volume *Around the World with General Grant*, written, with bland discretion, by a reporter for the *New York Herald* who accompanied the couple. But there were moments on the long odyssey that were more significant than those the reporter captured.

The Grants had to move out of the White House in March of 1877. They had lived in the house for eight years, and now they had nowhere they thought of as home to go to. The people of Galena and of Philadelphia had provided houses for the famous general and his lady, but neither spot seemed a place where they could comfortably settle down. As they got into the train at Washington's Union Station, Julia wept, saying, "I feel like a waif." "We're both waifs," replied her husband.[1] So, rather than settle anywhere, they chose nowhere. They were soon the country's best traveled, most famous waifs.

The opening chorus was a festive send-off, fireworks and all, as they set sail from Philadelphia on a June evening. They headed for England, where their daughter, Nellie, lived, but before they were through with their journey they had circumnavigated the globe and been greeted, as the advertisements for Wild West shows used to brag, by "The Crowned Heads of Europe"—and of Asia as well. And they had seen the sights—Egypt's pyramids, Pompeii in Italy, and India's Taj Mahal, in Agra. The scene designer couldn't have done better.

There was comedy—at Windsor Castle, with Queen Victoria as a wonderful walk-on. There were hints of tragedy of a bittersweet sort—Nellie Grant's fairy-tale White House wedding led to a marriage now gone sadly wrong. For grandeur, there were gloriously attired elephants to ride in India and wonderfully staged dances at the grand Siamese court. It was a glorious tourist adventure, but there were moments of reactions to Grant's career that were of considerable political significance. He and Julia together, simply by making the trip, carried much of America to a world only beginning to take their country's measure.

An unexpectedly large crowd cheered as Julia and Ulysses disem-

Pompeii.

1. Julia Grant, *Personal Memoirs*, 196–97.

ENTERING AGRA.

On the way to the Taj Mahal.

barked at Liverpool, and the attention showered on the short, stout American couple, so unheroic in appearance, proved to be a hero's welcome, one that was repeated again and again in city after city, country after country. It quickly got through to political grandees in England that the populace was impressed and reveling in entertaining the travelers. Soon even the Tories were vying with the Whigs for chances to fete the former president and Mrs. Grant. The American minister to Great Britain, Edwards Pierrepont, who had been in Grant's cabinet, gave a reception that left the chronicler of the trip running out of adjectives. When the Whig earl of Derby gave a grand reception for the Grants, the Tory Benjamin Disraeli, who had been skeptical of the whole business, was moved to give a luncheon. Grandest of all was the Lord Mayor's luncheon.

A summons to Windsor to meet the queen had to come next. But, as often happened in Grant's life, a triumphant moment slipped into comedy. Such invitations were much sought after, and though

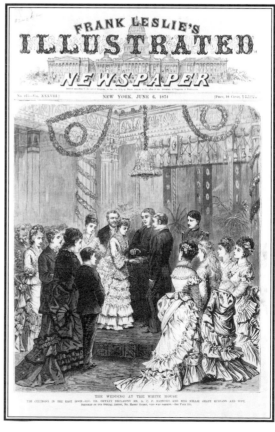

A White House wedding.

they might include a dinner and a night in the castle, they did not ensure meeting your hostess. If the queen was disinclined, she simply did not appear; for this occasion she was prepared to greet the Grants. But there was a hitch—of a particularly American kind. Three Grants, not two, turned up; Julia and Ulysses brought along their teenage son, Jesse. In the grander English houses this wasn't done. When the queen was told that the party of the guests of honor included a third person, a young third party, she called for her carriage and went for a drive; whereupon, a bevy of duchesses went to work trying to avert what was becoming an international incident.

Jesse refused one proposal that would have him eat with the household, a euphemism for the aristocrats that attended the queen, saying he would not "eat with the servants." The successful bit of diplomacy was to have two of Victoria's children join Jesse at the table. (Note the children in the formal picture of the queen's welcome to the Grants.)

RECEPTION AT WINDSOR BY THE QUEEN.

Queen Victoria did dine with her guests that evening and all passed civilly, but in her diary the next day, the queen noted that Jesse was a "very ill-mannered young Yankee."[2]

Few historians have noted the significance of the Grants' trip in introducing the United States to the world stage. The cosmopolitan politician-diplomats who went on to be presidents of the republic, John Adams and John Quincy Adams, Thomas Jefferson and James Monroe, had known Europe, and Europeans had known them. But most of their dealings had been with those at the head of governments and finance, and they had not brought the American presence to North Africa, the Middle East, or the great civilizations of Asia, as Grant was to do. To be sure, many other individuals opened the way for Americans to be known—missionaries reaching "heathen" lands throughout the nineteenth century, for example—but such emissaries did not carry the sense of the average American that, paradoxically, the famous general and former president and his lady did. There were more than enough heads of state to be met, but, in addition, huge crowds of the ordinary people of the globe saw and celebrated these Americans.

In some ways, Ulysses Grant resembled an earlier American performer on the European stage, Benjamin Franklin. Grant conducted no intricate diplomatic negotiations and, with an accompanying wife, there were no flirtatious aristocratic dalliances. But he was in every other way a match for his predecessor in portraying the simple American. What's more, unlike Franklin, Grant, or rather the Grants, took the message to an astonishingly large part of the world. Grant, traveling not as a head of state but as a private tourist, whom everyone knew to be a former president and, better, a great warrior, amassed a great deal of goodwill for his country. He was genuinely modest amid the grandeur of Europe, North Africa, India, Siam, and Japan.

One mysterious aspect of *Around the World with General Grant* is its failure to explain the Grants' relationship with their daughter, Nellie. Why, when they were nearby in England, did they spend so little time with their daughter and grandchild? Why were Nellie and her socially ambitious in-laws not at any of the glittering events in her parents' honor? While she was living in the White House, Nellie, at sixteen

---

2. Elizabeth Longford, *Queen Victoria: Born to Succeed* (New York: Harper and Row, 1965), 420.

OUR FIRST ELEPHANT RIDE.

The most impressive of the Grants' many modes of transportation.

and the apple of her indulgent father's eye, had been sent to London to be treated to the social whirl that a president's daughter could command. She was presented to the queen, and on shipboard, on the way back home, she met a charming Englishman named, almost too well, Algernon Sartoris. Julia Grant spared nothing in preparing the first White House wedding in decades, but at the ceremony, Nellie's father wept. He was right to have done so.

Nellie was taken by her husband, a member of a minor gentry family with major aspirations, to live in the south of England. Algernon's father had married one of the great opera stars of the day, Adelaide Kemble, who, in the familiar pattern, left the opera house on her marriage, never to sing in public again. She did, however, aspire to make something of her new daughter-in-law. Henry James, visiting the Sartorises in the country, noted that Adelaide was sure that Nellie "had natural aptitudes of every kind, and cannot sufficiently deplore the barbarous conduct of her mother leaving such excellent soil so perfectly untilled." In the country and at her house in London, Adelaide Sartoris (the sister of Fanny Kemble, the immensely popular actress) entertained the likes of Charles Dickens and Matthew Arnold. On one such occasion, Henry James noted that "poor little Nellie Grant sits speechless on the sofa, understanding neither head nor tail of such high discourse and exciting one's compassion for her incongruous lot in life."[3]

It was worse than a failure to grasp the world of the salon. The marriage began to sour. Nellie had gone to America and stayed with her parents in Long Branch when her first child was born. After returning to England, the infant died, the first in the trail of sad—and defeating—events that were to be Nellie's lot. She was with her parents for the birth of her second child (two more followed) just before they started their European trip. But the Grants, together, spent only one week with their daughter and infant grandchild at the Sartorises south coast place. It must have been an unhappy week, but we don't know why.

Soon the marriage began to unravel; everyone, including Henry James, spoke of Algernon Sartoris as if he were one of the useless gambling and drinking young men in Anthony Trollope's *The Way We Live*

3. Henry James to Alice James, May 19, [1879], in Leon Edel, ed., *The Letters of Henry James*, 2 vols. (Cambridge: Harvard University Press, 1974–75), 2:233.

Now, without specifying just what his particular version of cadishness was. By the time she was thirty, Nellie Grant Sartoris was a miserably unhappy woman. Her English family closed down on her. She and her children were the property of a wretched husband. When she came to America at the time of her father's fatal illness in 1885, she wrote for permission for her children to join her so that she could remain with her mother for the year after her father's death. Permission was not granted, and she went back to the children in England. It was five years before she could wrench herself and her children away, return permanently to America, and get a divorce.

That Julia and Ulysses Grant had little time for family matters was partly the fault of a dizzying round of receptions and formal banquets in England, which were matched as they proceeded around the globe. John Russell Young, the reporter accompanying the Grants and author of the two-volume *Around the World with General Grant*, writes of Grant leaving Brussels "having formed not only a high opinion of the character and sovereign of Belgium, but a personal friendship."[4] If Young is to be believed, Grant's judgment had deserted him. The king was Leopold II, who was embarking on what would be the virtual enslavement of the Congo. His tyrannical colonizing left a trail of horrors that would put the worst American slaveholder to shame, but, to be fair, when Grant met Leopold none of this had yet come fully to light. Young's polite, bland, yet chatty words telling of Leopold are typical of all of his assessments of the potentates the Grants met.

A plan to visit Paris was postponed when the American minister to France counseled that it would be unwise for Americans to appear to be influencing domestic politics in an upcoming election. The thinking was that Marshall Mac-Mahon, president of the Third Republic, but a monarchist, would surely greet Grant, and the handshake would be a rebuke to the republicans. Mac-Mahon had taken part in the ruthless suppression of the Paris Commune in 1871 and was anathema to republicans like Leon Gambetta, whom Grant much admired. Gambetta was determined to frustrate Mac-Mahon's attempt to return France to a monarchy, an effort that succeeded.

When the Grants, after ten days with Nellie, did reach Paris in

4. Young, *Around the World*, 1:47; recently reprinted as *Around the World with General Grant* by John Russell Young, Michael Fellman, editor (Baltimore, Md.: Johns Hopkins University Press, (2002).

October 1877, they took in the city's recent expression of opulence, the Paris Opera, but Julia did not pass up a visit to the ruling couturier, Worth, while the exhaustively diligent Paris filed a report that the general had been taken, via *"une porte secrete"* to observe some of the city's most spectacular dancers at the Bal Valentino. More publicly, there were stops in royal capitals from Madrid to St. Petersburg. Then it was

PAVILION OF THE OPERA.

Parisian splendor.

on to the Mediterranean. On one stop in Italy, a special archaeological dig was opened for them at Pompeii. In Rome, they met Pope Leo XIII and King Umberto. At sea, the party spent the time quietly on board the *Vandalia* with Mark Twain's *Innocents Abroad* as an excellent, if unorthodox, guidebook. Ulyss read the book aloud to Julia (her eyes always troubled her)—perhaps the sanest diversion possible not only from all the sight-seeing, banquets, and receptions they had endured and would endure, but also from the tedium of shipboard.

Christmas dinner 1877 took place on board the *Vandalia*, to Julia's

ON THE "SIMLA."

dclight. Arriving in Alexandria, in January 1878, the Grants savored the first "exotic" stop on their long journey. Egypt was much on the minds of the people of the Western world in the 1870s. The Suez Canal was opened in 1869, to the benefit of European imperialists. It caught the cultural eye as well. The canal's opening was celebrated, a little incongruously, with a production in Cairo of Verdi's *Rigoletto*, sent in to substitute for a yet unfinished opera set in Egypt. When it was completed in 1871, the triumphal *Aïda* opened in Milan. The Grants were treated to the full range of tourist fare, including a trip to the pyramids, and were received by the khedive, Ismail Pasha. From Egypt, the Grants made what was surely regarded as the most proper visit they could make, a stop at the Holy Land. Then it was back to Europe. Julia spent ten days with Nellie while Grant went to Ireland for a round of the now-customary formal receptions.

Surely the most spectacular portion of the Grants' itinerary was their long stay in Asia. In India, at the height of the Raj, Egypts' burros gave way to gorgeously bedecked elephants. Maharajas and Victo-

Ulysses on a mule in Egypt.

ENTERING SIOUT.

Julia had to make do with a pony.

ON THE WAY TO MEMPHIS.

VISIT TO THE KHEDIVE.

Egypt. West meets East.

ria's viceroy vied to provide the sumptuous entertainments for which the rich of the subcontinent were so famous. The Grants were feted to the point of exhaustion. By this time, his older brother Fred had replaced Jesse in the entourage. He eagerly went on a tiger hunt, while the general declined. (Blood sport had never been for him.)

In Siam (present-day Thailand), our musical joins another. King Chulalongkorn, Rama V (*below*), greeted Julia and Ulysses in impeccable British English. He had reigned since 1868, when, at fifteen, he succeeded his father, King Mongkut. It was Mongkut who had hired the

THE KING OF SIAM.

English governess Anna Leonowens to educate his sixty-seven children; her amazing memoir was the basis for *Anna and the King of Siam.* Just before her departure, the king, obviously fond of Anna, wrote her a note and closed it with the names of five favorites of her "affectionate students," among them Chulalongkorn. With three hours daily tutoring for over a year, Leonowens had seen to it that the prince would not be guilty of his father's wonderful malapropisms in English, quoted by Leonowens and repeated charmingly in the Rodgers and Hammerstein musical based on Margaret Landon's book.

The Grants were received at the palace and given a banquet, at which Grant had his own message for the sovereign. In his formal toast to the king at the banquet, Grant urged him to send Siamese young men to study in the United States. The idea, if good, was not a practical one. It would have been difficult for a Siamese student to overcome the limits of language and of resistance to Asians in the United States.

RECEPTION OF GENERAL GRANT BY THE KING.

One of dozens of vast formal dinners.

The next stop was Cochin China and Saigon. Again, they were greeted, if not royally, certainly grandly. Their pleasant departure was taken scarcely a century before a far less graceful American exodus from the city—from Vietnam and its war. Off to Singapore, with its clamorous port, to Hong Kong, and then to Canton, in China.

Certainly one of the most incongruous conveyances that Grant endured was the sedan chair in which he was carried by a team of hefty bearers to the viceroy's palace in China. A sizable crowd of curious city people viewed the grandees at feed at Prince Kung's banquet, outdoors under lanterns. Describing the banquet, John Russell Young treats himself to a lengthy would-be humorous description of bizarre dishes—bird's-nest soup comes in for particular wit—that he was certain would seem totally strange and equally amusing for his readers. Were it set in columns on laminated cardboard, his prose would be a menu familiar to nine out of ten of his fellow New Yorkers a century later.

And, finally, exhaustedly, Japan. The Meiji, the emperor who the

COALING AT SINGAPORE.

Another side of the story.

THE PROCESSION TO THE VICEROY'S.

INTERVIEW WITH PRINCE KUNG.

year before had finally consolidated his power by putting down the shoguns that had governed Japan, and embarked on the Westernizing of his country, warmly greeted the Grants. Shaking Ulysses Grant's hand, he signaled his welcome to the man who had put down a very different rebellion in his own country. Young's reportorial skill does not falter as he describes a vast military parade viewed by the emperor and a privately uneasy General Grant, who found military pomp distasteful.

The immense public celebrations of every sort that the Grants had been treated to, had endured, obscured two events that speak to the most serious side of Grant and his accomplishments. The two, early in the trip, stood in stark relief to each other. They underscored contradictory outcomes of Grant's Civil War. The first took place in Newcastle, a grim industrial city in the north of England. The cast, too big for the biggest stage, was composed of eighty thousand working-class Britons who had organized to fight the cruel effects of the relentless Industrial Revolution. There were conditions to complain of—children working in mines, potters dying of lead poisoning—that American slave owners had once made a point of saying their slaves did not have to endure. This was not how the laborers in Newcastle saw it. Peacefully struggling for emancipation from a suppressive class system, they turned out to celebrate the man who, with a war, had emancipated a working class in his own country.

Grant was one of them, a cousin, and they loved him for what he had, in their eyes, accomplished. Karl Marx had made the connection; the Union cause had been the freeing of workers. Few Americans, including black Americans, described the process with this rhetoric, but it was never absent from black Americans' minds that the true reason for the war, the great accomplishment of the war, was their emancipation.

The men and women of Newcastle remembered that the war had been about emancipation, while white Americans, at the close of Reconstruction, were energetically forgetting the fact. Crowds jammed the railway station and adjacent streets as the Grants came in from Edinburgh, and the guests of honor were treated to the usual routine— a tour of a castle, a luncheon with the chamber of commerce—which offered no clue as to what the next day would bring. On September 22, 1877, Grant was escorted to a field on the outskirts of town.

I know of no way to describe the day in Newcastle better than to

MEETING THE EMPEROR IN THE SUMMER-HOUSE.

ADDRESS AT NEWCASTLE

quote the local newspaper. Its account belies the silk hats in the picture from Young's book (*above*). From all over the North Country, by train, wagon, or on foot they poured into the city and the great parade began: "Then came the Durham Miners' Association, carrying a blue silk banner, bearing a design which represented the change in the condition of the pitboys, by the introduction of short hours of labor; the Hepworth and Ravensworth colliers, carrying a blue silk banner, representing the union of capital and labor, a coal owner and workman in friendly conversation, with the legend, 'Reason, Truth, and Friendship.' . . . Another showed a figure representing emancipation, and the tree of union in full bloom. Another banner, of blue silk with yellow border, contained the words, 'We claim manhood suffrage.' [Grant must have been reminded of the Fifteenth Amendment, which he had thought had guaranteed this back home.] . . . Then came the Hammermen's Society, the Plumbers, the House Furnishers, and Tanners of Elswick. The latter carried a banner bearing these words: 'Welcome back, General Grant, from Arms to Arts,' 'Let us have Peace,' 'Nothing like leather.' [Working men in America in 1872 had campaigned for Grant and his vice presidential candidate, Henry Wilson, under the slogan 'Tanner and Tailor'; Grant had hated his father's tannery, and Wilson hadn't sewed a suit in a good many years, but it brought in votes.] The Masons, the independent Order of Mechanics, the Newcastle Brass Moulders and Finishers, the Tyne District Carpenters and Joiners, and Mill Sawyers and Machinists followed. . . . [T]here was no disturbance of the peace, and a few policemen kept the line."[5]

When Grant replied to the welcoming speech of a spokesman of the "working classes," he said that wars, when they come, "fall upon the many, the producing class, who are the sufferers," the class that furnishes the things of war for those "engaged in destroying and not producing."[6]

The second event, a scene in Berlin, seemed worlds away. There, in an office in a vast palace, two men talked of the outcome of the American Civil War and of the creation of two potentially powerful and united nation-states—Germany and the United States. The men were Chancellor Otto von Bismarck, whose mighty Germany would one day do terrible damage in the world, and Ulysses S. Grant, who, unwittingly, was responsible for enabling his America to one day gain the awesome strength it has today. The visit began when Grant left his hotel, cigar in hand, and walked over to the imposing Radziwell Palace and into the courtyard, tossing away the stump of his cigar. Uniformed guards, expecting an entourage of carriages, belatedly threw open the vast doors and with exquisite grandeur showed the president and general in to the presence of Chancellor Bismarck.

---

5. *Newcastle Daily Chronicle*, September 24, 1877, quoted in McFeely, *Grant: A Biography*, 461.
6. McFeely, *Grant: A Biography*, 462.

Bismarck immediately struck a friendly note, complimenting Grant on how young and fit he was. (He was a healthy fifty-six.) They then talked of a mutual acquaintance, Philip H. Sheridan, a young general to whom Grant had given great responsibility during the Civil War and who had been to Europe to witness and admire the success of the Prussian army during the 1870 Franco-Prussian War. Admiration of Sheridan spoke to the militaristic turn of mind of the two men. Turning to Grant's achievement in the war, Bismarck was more impressed by the restoration of the union than the freeing of the slaves. " 'Yes,' said the prince, 'you had to save the Union just as we had to save Ger-

MEETING WITH BISMARCK.

many.' 'Not only to save the Union, but destroy slavery,' answered the General. 'I suppose, however, that the Union was the real sentiment, the dominant sentiment' said the prince. 'In the beginning, yes,' said the General, "but as soon as slavery fired upon the flag it was felt, we all felt, even those who did not object to slaves, that slavery must be destroyed. We felt that it was a stain to the Union that men should be bought and sold like cattle.' "[7]

As the meeting ended, Grant commented favorably on the Congress of Berlin of 1878, then in session. The two men were, in effect, taking cognizance of the fact that the unity of two great nation-states had been achieved through their agency. Neither man could have known to what uses the power of his now firmly united country would be put—for good and for hideous harm.

The union on which Bismarck congratulated Grant has led to arrogance, as, a century later, American has amassed power that has outstripped even that which Bismarck unleashed in Germany. But the strengthening of the union has had a positive effect as well. By destroying a rebellion of states and supporting the three Reconstruction amendments to the Constitution, Grant laid the cornerstone for a union still not fully built. Grant had helped create federal power with the potential of bringing equality to the entire population of the United States. The exercise of this power was used to good effect during the Civil Rights movement, the second Reconstruction that the failure of the first made necessary. The present-day diminishing of this federal power in favor of a return to states rights' particularism threatens to diminish Grant's two greatest achievements: the ending of slavery that his war accomplished and the creation—not simply the restoration— of a union powerful enough to tend to the needs of all its citizens.

There was as well a twenty-first-century dimension to Grant's trip. "Globalization" is on every tongue today. Europe had been the training ground for eighteenth-century politicians who would go on to be presidents—John Adams and Thomas Jefferson, as well as James Monroe and John Quincy Adams. Preparation for the presidency resided on our own continent with the ascendancy of Andrew Jackson. America's attention—and the White House's—was off Europe and on our own mainland. Until Woodrow Wilson went to Europe after World War I,

7. Young, *Around the World*, 1:416.

and was criticized for it, no sitting president traveled abroad. Ulysses Grant, a highly visible ex-president, was a global pioneer.

Commodore Matthew Perry introduced the West to Japan and Japan to the West in the 1850s; it was only a quarter of a century later when the Grants followed him there. Unlike Perry, who had a single mission, gaining access to Japan, Grant, with no goal other than to be a tourist, was nevertheless adding critically to the opening of the world's eyes. Unofficially he was America's ambassador without portfolio. He let a remarkably large portion of the globe see a remarkably typical American.

When the moment came to leave Japan, with plans to visit Australia abandoned, the Grant party's boat was laden with a vast collection of gifts from their plethora of hosts around the world. A swarm of boats in the harbor formally saw the Grants off for their trip across the Pacific—and home. The American couple arrived safely in home port—this time San Francisco—back, in a sense, where they started. But America had not stood still while they were away. Reconstruction was firmly over, to black Americans' great detriment; labor unrest in the North had been put down by force; and the moneygrubbing of the Gilded Age—unmatched until our own time—was in full swing. But for the moment, all of that was obscured beneath a rousing American celebration, bunting and tableaux and the chorus in full voice with its "Welcome Grant." The waifs were home.

THE ARRIVAL AT SAN FRANCISCO.

7

Grant's Book

Personal Memoirs of
U. S. Grant

The writing of the *Personal Memoirs of U. S. Grant* was by any measure a remarkable feat. The 1880s were perplexing years for Grant. Back from the trip with Julia around the world, he failed to be nominated for a third term in 1880 (more to Julia's distress than his). He negotiated a trade agreement with Mexico at President Chester A. Arthur's bidding and dabbled in a railroad scheme, the Mexican Southern Railroad (a venture strikingly like the fiasco at the center of Trollope's 1875 *The Way We Live Now*, his satire of Victorian society) but found nothing to fully engage his attention. He and Julia moved into a town house on East Sixty-sixth Street in New York City, a city that they did not know well.

There Grant set out on the last of the business enterprises for which he had no aptitude, that of an investment banker. With Fernando Ward, a man well known on Wall Street, Ulysses Jr. had started a brokerage house, and he brought his father, the former president, into the business as a lure for customers. Thanks to the business naïveté of father and son and to the crookedness of their partner, the firm failed amid a classic Wall Street scandal enlivened by the fame of one of the fallen. Grant had to turn to William Henry Vanderbilt for a loan to meet his creditors. Vanderbilt also took possession of the potpourri of gifts the Grants had brought back from their trip around the world in order to keep these out of the hands of other creditors. (The trove is in the Smithsonian Institution today.)

In 1884, Grant was once again reduced almost to poverty. He had to find a way to provide for himself and for Julia. Civil War generals writing of their exploits was a standard literary outpouring of the day, and *Century Magazine* engaged Grant to write two articles for five hundred dollars each. This surely would not provide the wherewithal to solve his problem, but it put him on a path that would. *Century*, on the basis of the articles, wanted a full memoir and proposed a contract. When Grant's friend Samuel Clemens (a.k.a. Mark Twain) heard about the offer, he trumped it with his own—one with an advance and a generous royalty.

Grant set to work. What resulted was Grant's book, a memoir not as a richly detailed account of the personal side of the writer's life, but rather as a narrative that enables us to take stock of the intellect, even the character, of the author. If the book is a superior piece of military history—essentially an account of two wars, the Mexican and for most of the two volumes the Civil War—the subject is Grant himself against the backdrop of war.

It is correct to say that the impetus was to provide for Julia (after his death she received a royalty check for two hundred thousand dollars, a record for the day; Clemens made out still better). But the book became much more than that. Grant had barely set to work when he was diagnosed—after a possibly fatal delay in treatment—as having cancer of the esophagus. In the next ten months, his writing not only pushed dying aside, but also wiped out the final remaining evidence of Ulysses Grant as a failure. In this astonishingly short time he produced a two-volume work of literary distinction. The energy to bring it through to victory was borrowed from his subject. War had aroused in him a relentless determination to succeed; reliving that war drove him forward with no less determination to complete his book. Giving definition to his war, he defined himself.

It was patriotic and respectable to have the two thick green-bound

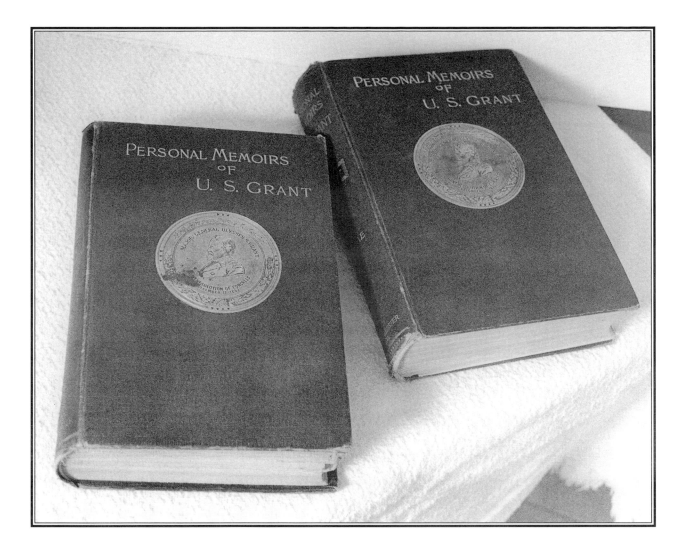

volumes on your parlor table in the year after Grant died. Something else must account for the admiration that the book has attracted in the decades since it was published. Mark Twain (page 130) called the book the finest writing by a military commander since Julius Caesar's *Commentaries*, but his blurb has to be discounted since he was Grant's publisher. (Mark Twain, having saved Grant from a stingy book contract, got in the bargain the *Memoirs* as the second book on his own new publishing company's list. The other was *The Adventures of Huckleberry Finn*.)

The ranking critic of the day, Matthew Arnold, had a good many

reservations—Grant was, after all, an American and had trouble with his *that*s and *which*es—but the lofty British critic came to admire the work. Later critics—each with as distinct a voice as Mark Twain's and Arnold's—have sung the book's praises in the decades since: Gertrude Stein, Edmund Wilson, and Gore Vidal, none of whom, surely, is of the usual run of Grant fans.

I think one of the things that brought these three unique critical voices, spanning the twentieth century, to an appreciation of Grant's prose was that he too speaks with his own voice. Grant's writing is unlike most of the writers to which he is regularly compared. A good many generals of the Civil War, Union and Confederate, wrote their memoirs. More often than not these memoirs are more or less a cataloging of their doings in the war, often with long, skippable passages from official dispatches. Many times the purpose was to exonerate themselves for any failure, transferring the blame not to the foe, but to fellow officers fighting on the same side. Edmund Wilson, in his famous collection of essays on Civil War literature, *Patriotic Gore*, credits William Tecumseh Sherman in his memoir with displaying vividly his choleric personality and with writing sentences that you can almost hear pouring from the ones preceding it. But Sherman does not sustain his narrative with the quiet orderly force Grant brought to his book.

Gertrude Stein in *Four in America* (essays on Grant, Wilbur Wright, Henry James, and George Washington), with characteristic perversity, likens Grant to a religious leader and James to a general. You have to go to the James essay to get the question "What do generals do." And the answer: "Of course generals do do something." What was that something? "So then if Henry James had been a general what would he have had to have done. This which he did do."[1] The "this" that James did, of course, was write. And, if Grant did what he did, wage war, he is also being a proper general when he writes his *Memoirs*. Stein does not explicitly say that war is an American religion, but she implies it. Grant, known correctly as a leader in war, is, she insists, a religious leader. If so, his *Memoirs* is that religion's Bible.

Edmund Wilson quotes with pleasure Grant's put-down, worthy of Mark Twain, of a minister who complained to him about battles being fought on Sabbath. The general explained that it was unavoidable, to which the minister reiterated that it was unfortunate. "'Yes, very unfortunate,' admitted Grant. 'Every effort should be made to respect the Sabbath day, and it is exceedingly gratifying to know that it is observed so generally throughout the country.'" Wilson, though nicely aware of Grant's skepticism (and wit), curiously follows a train of thought similar to Stein's: "The completely non-religious Sherman once paid him the very strange compliment" that fighting under the General's command could be likened " 'to nothing else than the faith a Christian had in his Savior.' " Wilson then sees in the *Memoirs* why it was that Grant

---

1. Gertrude Stein, *Four in America* (New Haven: Yale University Press, 1947), 136–37.

inspired such confidence, crediting him with "a natural fineness of character, mind and taste," as well as with having "dynamic force." Then the great critic adds, "Perhaps never has a book so objective in form seemed so personal in every line."[2]

Wilson sees Grant's "calm" narrative rising to only two peaks. The taking of Vicksburg midway through the war falls neatly in volume 1. This is balanced by the story of the war's end at Appomattox in volume 2. I would add others: Grant's excitement at the news of Sherman's capture of Atlanta, which produced his generous letter to his more flamboyant colleague, for example. Here and several other times the steadfastness of the prose is allowed to burst its bounds.

A more or less random passage from his book, one that does indeed anticipate Vicksburg, may best suggest the driving force of Grant's narrative. The general has spent frustrating months trying to find a way to take that crucial little city, which stands on a steep bluff above the Mississippi River and commands passage along the river. By the spring of 1863, Grant has gotten his troops below the city and is advancing on his goal from behind. Crossing tributaries of the Mississippi, he has reached almost to Grand Gulf, a small port south of Vicksburg. Midway through his chapter, he writes:

> During the night of the 2[d] of May the bridge over the North Fork was repaired, and the troops commenced crossing at five the next morning. Before the leading brigade was over it was fired upon by the enemy from a commanding position; but they were soon driven off. It was evident that the enemy was covering a retreat from Grand Gulf to Vicksburg. Every commanding position from this (Grindstone) crossing to Hankinson's ferry over the Big Black was occupied by the retreating foe to delay our progress. McPherson, however, reached Hankinson's ferry before night, seized the ferry boat, and sent a detachment of his command across and several miles north on the road to Vicksburg. When the junction of the road going to Vicksburg with the road from Grand Gulf to Raymond and Jackson was reached, Logan with his division was turned to the left towards

2. Edmund Wilson, *Patriotic Gore: Studies in the Literature of the American Civil War* (New York: Oxford University Press, 1962), 141, 142, 143.

Grand Gulf. I went with him a short distance from this junction. McPherson had encountered the largest force yet met since the battle of Port Gibson and had a skirmish nearly approaching a battle; but the road Logan had taken enabled him to come up on the enemy's right flank, and they soon gave way. McPherson was ordered to hold Hankinson's ferry and the road back back to Willow Springs with one division; McClernand, who was now in the rear, was to join in this as well as to guard the line back down the bayou. I did not want to take the chances of having an enemy lurking in our rear.

On the way from the junction to Grand Gulf, where the road comes into the one from Vicksburg to the same place six or seven miles out, I learned that the last of the enemy had retreated past that place on their way to Vicksburg. I left Logan to make the proper disposition of his troops for the night, while I rode into the town with an escort of about twenty cavalry. Admiral Porter had already arrived with his fleet. The enemy had abandoned his heavy guns and evacuated the place.

When I reached Grand Gulf May 3[d] I had not been with my baggage since the 27th of April and consequently had had no change of underclothing, no meal except such as I could pick up sometimes at other headquarters, and no tent to cover me. The first thing I did was to get a bath, borrow some fresh underclothing from one of the naval officers and get a good meal on the flag-ship. Then I wrote letters to the general-in-chief informing him of our present position, dispatches to be telegraphed from Cairo, orders to General Sullivan commanding above Vicksburg, and gave orders to all my corps commanders. About twelve o'clock at night I was through my work and started for Hankinson's ferry, arriving there before daylight.[3]

On reading this, your first instinct is to want a map in motion that shows where Grant and his armies are; your second is to realize you don't need it. With a remarkable ability to see it all in his mind's eye and, what's more, to communicate the picture to his readers, he has

3. U. S. Grant, *Personal Memoirs,* 1:489.

drawn the map for you. Maps, after all, are static, and movement is what Grant's story here is all about. Grant's visual sense together with his awareness that war is always a matter of unexpected change had much to do with his enormous success as a military commander. Similarly, you don't even have to have the McPhersons and Logans identified to sense what these two generals' men are doing and where they are going. The author has made clarity out of what at the time must have been a mystery to the hundreds of his men on the move and even his less adroit generals. Without a backward glance, he abandoned what had been his plan in the morning and shifted his armies to ready them for the next day.

And before you is Grant's astonishing energy. It is in vivid contrast to the torpor that you can sense in so many instances in his life before the war, and after it. With a hint of the importance of his naval allies in this campaign, Grant also gives a nod to the navy for providing a very personal need, clean underwear. We can almost see and smell a very human warrior. Bathed, dressed, and fed, he is on his horse again at midnight to ride through the night. He has become a vivid character in his story.

In the next passage from the one quoted, Grant underscores another of his traits: the ability to adjust to the inevitable changes that a vast war entails. Another general, Nathaniel Banks, operating farther down the Mississippi and on his way to reinforce Grant's armies, is not moving as Grant expected him to. "To wait for his cooperation could have detained me at least a month," Grant writes.[4] To wait at Grand Gulf for General Banks would be to give the enemy time to bring in reinforcements greater than those Banks would have provided. What's more, Grant was in no mood for waiting.

Plans, in his mind, were always a matter of change; he gave up his idea of using Grand Gulf as his base of operation. Instead, he would risk both losing a secure source of supplies to feed his large armies and incurring (once again) the wrath of the chief of staff in Washington, General Henry Wager Halleck, whom he knew would advise caution. Even General Sherman (who, famously, was to do the same thing as he began his march through Georgia) advised that Grant not cut himself off from his source of supply and communication. But Grant had none of it; he was on the move. Giving new orders, he led his armies directly

4. Ibid.

to the rear of Vicksburg and began the siege that resulted, in July 1863, in the fall of the city and the Union's command of the Mississippi.

You can be certain that those orders were succinct, brief, and clear. In the summer of 1864, halted at his headquarters at City Point, Virginia, Grant wrote perhaps six or seven important orders a day moving armies all across the almost continental range of the Civil War. All are clear—his control of syntax is superb—and all are in the same steady hand that produced in his *Memoirs* a narrative of virtually the entire war.

Edmund Wilson observes correctly that there is virtually no mention in Grant's *Personal Memoirs* of the war's casualties. Like Lincoln, Grant was aware of the winning calculus that if he simply did not have more casualties than did the Confederates, the North would win the war. Demographics were with him; there were more men to be had for the Union army than for the South, which would eventually run out of men to fight. In one unusual use of metaphor, Grant tells of the dead on a field at Shiloh being so plentiful that they were as close as stepping-stones across a creek. But that is as close to war's horror as Grant would allow himself to get.

Wilson regards the *Memoirs* as "a unique expression of the national character,"[5] much as *Leaves of Grass* and *Walden* are. With Grant there is always the sense that he will never seem to be over-reaching himself. Enormous energy, even ambition, may lurk under his calm, simple demeanor, but that demeanor is genuine. He does not, either in his life or his prose, ever put on a show. It has always seemed to me that he knew exactly what he was doing when he wore his simple unbuttoned blue jacket to receive the surrender of the resplendent Robert E. Lee. That was what he wore every day on his job; what else would he wear? And by his choice, he fits the American mode. With Grant it was not artifice. One of the secrets to his great success as a commander in his American war was that his men, rather than standing in perhaps resentful awe, identified with him. They trusted him, and followed him. He achieved his masterful leadership without show, a manner that he carried into his book's prose. In all of the one thousand pages there is not a flourish.

On one point Wilson is quite wrong. Nicely irreverent about war, he denies that waging it could have had as a goal a societal gain. Grant

---

5. Wilson, *Patriotic Gore*, 133.

made clear in his explanation to Bismarck that slavery was ended because slavery was wrong and not simply as an expedient in a tussle for power. Wilson misses the key point. Grant said, "slavery," not Confederates, not Southerners, "fired on the flag." It was not the twentieth-century critic—who seems scarcely to have noticed black Americans, the most interested parties in the war's outcome—but the Civil War general who understood that slavery, the institution, and the Confederacy, its home, were synonymous.

In light of the subsequent national abandonment of the black Americans who had been slaves, Wilson may be correct to be cynical. His famous metaphor for the war is "a primitive organism called a sea slug gobbling up smaller organisms through a large orifice at one end of its body; confronted with another sea slug of only slightly lesser size, ingurgitates that, too."[6] Edmund Wilson's vivid image for the Civil War, perhaps for all war, fits a power-hungry late-twentieth- or, even more, twenty-first-century America better than it fits Grant's America. It was a failure of the vaunted American democracy that we failed to end slavery without resorting to war, but when we did turn to war, Grant knew that ending it was his job. If President Grant was unable to achieve total victory for the freed people in what passed for peace in the region in which most former slaves lived, General Grant, in 1878 correcting Bismarck, remembered, correctly, what he had been fighting for. He said as much when he wrote in the conclusion of *Personal Memoirs* that slavery was the war's cause.

Ironically, Grant, who is often credited with having written the most distinguished memoir of any ex-president, says almost nothing about his presidency. He has been much criticized for his job as president. (For the wrong reasons; his failure was more in not accomplishing more for the former slaves than in countenancing some blatant corruption by his cabinet members.) Grant worked on the *Memoirs* chronologically, but his postwar years get short shrift. The book ends abruptly, due in part almost surely to the increasing amount of morphine he was taking for his pain. But I am not sure that he wasn't just as happy that he did not have to dwell on this time in his life. It was the wars, particularly the Civil War, that had truly engaged him.

Grant was still editing the last of the manuscript within two weeks

6. Ibid., xi.

of his death on July 23, 1885. With the best of misguided intentions, his son Fred and presumably Julia urged him to finish so that he could live out the end of his life comfortably at rest. Work, not rest, was what sustained him. They failed to see that Grant's life had become his book; when it was finished, so was he.

Acknowledgments

We are extremely grateful to the many archivists that have supplied the images for this book. A few pictures that we ordered could not, for one reason or another, be used, but we are no less appreciative of the archivists who sent us these. A list of pictures and credits is on the following pages.

A special word of thanks to Maja Keech of the Library of Congress, who not only led us through their vast collection, but also was enthusiastic about the project from the first. Many people in the Harvard University libraries were helpful. Martha Mahard was the excellent sleuth who tracked doctored photographs used for the steel engravings in Civil War newspapers, Joe Bourneuf provided excellent detective work on a worrisome quotation, and Robert Zwinck did a masterful job of photographing nineteenth-century material.

As usual, the people at W. W. Norton were great to work with. Sarah Stewart got the project started, Jeannie Luciano did the essential moving and shaking to keep it going when Sarah left, Andy Marasia has, once again, been willing to face up to Grant, and Ann Tappert did the fine copyediting of the manuscript. Jason Baskin has adroitly run interference through the maze that is Norton. I owe my greatest thanks to Bob Weil, a nicely demanding editor. It was he who put me in touch with Neil Giordano, who is not only a first-rate photographic editor, but also fun to work with.

Gloria Watts was an eagle-eyed proofreader, and, as ever, Mary Drake McFeely was an indispensible critic and editor.

W. S. M.

Illustrations
and Credits

Chapter 1: "Attributed to Slavery"

pp. 2 and 10, Unidentified black soldier, Chicago Historical Society, ICHi-22166; p. 4, Simon Bolivar Buckner, Kentucky Historical Society, Special Collections and Archives; p. 5, "The Surrender of Fort Donelson," from *Harper's Weekly*, March 1, 1862, Courtesy of Widener Library, Harvard University; p. 8, Hardscrabble, Library of Congress, LC-USZ62-088517; p. 9, Fort Vancouver, Washington Territory, Library of Congress, LC-USZ62-31252; p. 10, Soldier with slave pens, Richmond, Virginia, Library of Congress, LC-B871-2299; p. 11, "Officers and crew of the gunboat *Mendota*," Widener Library; p. 12, "Laborers at the Alexandria Wharf," Widener Library; p. 13, "The War on the Mississippi" ("Negroes at Work on the Canal"), from *Harper's Weekly*, March 1863, Widener Library; p. 14, Woman in front of cabin, Library of Congress, LC-USZ62-16362; p. 15, Family of former slaves, photograph by Timothy O'Sullivan, Library of Congress, LC-B8171-152-A; p. 15, "Freedmen's Village," Widener Library; p. 16, Group portrait of ex-slaves, Library of Congress, LC-B8171-383; p. 17, "'Zion' School for Colored Children, Charleston, South Carolina," from *Harper's Weekly*, Library of Congress, LC-USZ62-117666; p. 18, "Electioneering at the South," from *Harper's Weekly*, Library of Congress, LC-USZ62-29235; p. 19, Portrait of Grant by Matthew Brady, Library of Congress, LC-B8172-6371; p. 21, Portrait of a John A. Rawlins, Library of Congress, LC-BH82 4431; pp. 22–24, Political cartoons, Library of Congress, LC-USZ62-24938 ("Grant's New War Horse"), LC-USZ62-32499 ("The Constitutional Amendment"), LC-USZ62-

40861 ("The Black Vomit"); pp. 26, 27, Grant at Mount McGregor, Library of Congress, LC-USZ62-7607, LC-USZ62-10453.

Chapter 2: A Love Story

p. 28, Grant family portrait, Library of Congress, LC-USZ62-092450; p. 31, Ulysses S. Grant at twenty-one, Library of Congress; p. 33, Arabian horse, Library of Congress, LC-USZ62-92741; p. 34, Pawn receipt, Illinois State Historical Library; p. 35, Nellie and Jesse Grant, Chicago Historical Society; p. 36, Nellie Grant, Chicago Historical Society; p. 37, Fred Grant, United States Military Academy Library, Special Collections; p. 40, White House dining room, Library of Congress, LC-USZ62-094242; p. 41, Hamilton and Julia Fish, Library of Congress, LC-USZ62-37517, LC-USZ62-127506; p. 43, Julia Dent Grant, Library of Congress, LC-USZ62-101567; p. 45, White House, from *Harper's Weekly*, Library of Congress, LC-USZ62-127061; p. 45, White Haven, Missouri Historical Society, Prints and Photographs Department.

Chapter 3: Presenting a General

pp. 47 and 56, Grant standing with his war horse "Cincinnati," Library of Congress, LC-USZ62-101396; p. 49, Grant oak, Library of Congress, LC-USZ62-127504; p. 50, "The Hero of Fort Donelson," from *Harper's Weekly*, March 8, 1862, Widener Library; p. 51, Composite 1862 portrait, Library of Congress, LC-USZ62-110716; p. 53, Studio portrait by Matthew Brady, Library of Congress, LC-B8184-10567; p. 54, "Lieut.-Gen. Ulysses S. Grant, U.S.A.," centerfold from *Leslie's Illustrated*, March 19, 1864, Widener Library; p. 55, Grant at City Point, photograph by Matthew Brady, Library of Congress, LC-B8184-B76; p. 55, Grant at City Point, *Harper's Weekly* engraving, Library of Congress, LC-USZ62-108023; p. 57, Composite photograph of Grant on horseback at City Point, Library of Congress, LC-USZ62-21992; p. 58, Grant by C. W. Reed, Library of Congress, LC-USZ62-95560; p. 58, Statue by Daniel Chester French and Edward Clark Potter, Library of Congress, LC-USZ62-085379; p. 59, Grant by N. C. Wyeth, Library of Congress, LC-USZ62-71918; p. 60, Detail of Henry Merwin Shrady statue, Library of Congress, LC-USZ62-32220; p. 61, Full statue by Shrady, Library of Congress, LC-USF34-060435-D; p. 62, Shaw Memorial (detail), photograph by Neil Giordano; p. 63, Grant standing portrait, Library of Congress, LC-USZ62-084561.

Chapter 4: "No Pen Portray"

pp. 64 and 71, "The Siege of Petersburg," from *Leslie's Illustrated*, September 2, 1864; p. 66, "The Storming of Fort Donelson," Currier and Ives print, Library of Congress, LC-USZ62-16919; p. 67, S. B. Buckner, Library of Congress, LC-USZ62-079789; p. 68, Column from *Harper's Weekly*, March 1, 1862, Widener Library; p. 69, "Admiral Porter's Fleet Running the Rebel Blockade of the Mississippi at Vicksburg, April 16th, 1863," Currier and Ives print, Library of Congress, LC-USZ62-30; p. 69, "The War in East Tennessee," from *Harper's Weekly*, November 21, 1863, Widener Library; p. 70, "Grant's Campaign in Virginia," from *Leslie's Illustrated*, July 2, 1864, Widener Library; p. 71, "Grant's Movements South of the James," from *Leslie's Illustrated*, October 22, 1864, Widener Library; p. 73, Dead soldier at Antietam by Alexander Gardner, Library of Congress, LC-B871-726; pp. 74–75, *Gardner's Photographic Sketchbook of the War*, cover, Plate 66, and Plate 50, Widener Library; p. 78, Robert W. Weir, Widener Library.

Chapter 5: Havens and Houses

pp. 81 and 95, " 'Reb' and 'Billy Burton' Carrying the President's Children to School," from *Harper's Weekly*, Library of Congress, USZ62-37342, p. 84, Christmas dinner aboard the *Vandalia*, from John Russell Young's *Around the World with General Grant*, Widener Library; p. 84, White Haven, Missouri Historical Society, Prints and Photographs Department; p. 85, Point Pleasant, Ohio, Library of Congress, LC-USZ62-23789; p. 85, Georgetown, Ohio, Library of Congress, LC-USZ62-32875; p. 86, Georgetown schoolhouse, Library of Congress, LC-USZ62-127507, p. 87, West Point, from above Washington Valley, Library of Congress, LC USZ62-1077; p. 87, "Army of Occupation at Corpus Christi, Texas," Widener Library; p. 88, Detroit residence, Library of Congress, LC-USZ62-32878; p. 89, Fort Vancouver residence, Library of Congress, HABS WASH 6-VANCO 1-B-1; p. 90, Hardscrabble interior photographs, Library of Congress, LC-USZ62-32873, LC-USZ62-32892; pp. 91, 92, Galena harness shop and Galena house, Courtesy of Galena/Jo Daviess County Historical Society and Museum; p. 93, Galena postwar house, Library of Congress, LC-USZ62-12287; p. 94, Grant, Julia, and Jesse at City Point, Library of Congress, LC-B8184-10267; pp. 95, 96, "President Grant's Cottage at Long Branch," from *Harper's Weekly*, August 13, 1870, and New York City E. 66th St. town house, Courtesy of the Picture Collection, The Branch Libraries, The New York Public Library, Astor, Lenox and Tilden Foundations; p. 97, Mount McGregor, Library of Congress, LC-USZ62-36978; p. 98, Grant family portrait at Mount McGregor, Library of Congress, LC-USZ62-38103; p. 99, Grant's tomb, Library of Congress, LC-USZ62-1817.

Chapter 6: Waifs Abroad

All illustrations reproduced from John Russell Young's *Around the World with General Grant*, courtesy of Widener Library, except the following: p. 103, "The Wedding at the White House," from *Leslie's Illustrated*, June 6, 1874, Library of Congress, LC-USZ62-094003; and p. 125, "Welcome Grant," Library of Congress, LC-USZ62-127505.

Chapter 7: Grant's Book

p. 126, Grant at Mount McGregor, Library of Congress, LC-USZ62-7607; p. 129, Covers of *Personal Memoirs*, photograph by Mary McFeely; p. 130, Mark Twain, Library of Congress, LC-USZ62-08536; p. 137, Grant family at Mount McGregor, Library of Congress, LC-USZ62-21900.